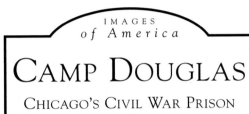

IMAGES
of America

CAMP DOUGLAS
CHICAGO'S CIVIL WAR PRISON

On the cover: **OVERCROWDING AT CAMP DOUGLAS.** Camp Douglas was the nation's deadliest Civil War prison. (Courtesy of the Chicago History Museum.)

IMAGES
of America

CAMP DOUGLAS
CHICAGO'S CIVIL WAR PRISON

Kelly Pucci

ARCADIA
PUBLISHING

Published by Arcadia Publishing
Charleston SC, Chicago IL, Portsmouth NH, San Francisco CA

Printed in the United States of America

Library of Congress Catalog Card Number: 2007934437

For all general information contact Arcadia Publishing at:
Telephone 843-853-2070
Fax 843-853-0044
E-mail sales@arcadiapublishing.com
For customer service and orders:
Toll-Free 1-888-313-2665

Visit us on the Internet at www.arcadiapublishing.com

CONTENTS

ACKNOWLEDGMENTS

The author gratefully acknowledges the work of all Camp Douglas historians, especially Andrew M. Greeley, George Levy, and Jim Barr.

Special thanks go to the staff of the Chicago Public Library, especially to Teresa Yoder and Lyle Benedict. Thanks also go to the staff of the Chicago History Museum, especially to Erin Tikovitsch for scanning photographs.

For additional photograph contributions the author thanks the following: Joan C. McKinney of the Campbellsville University; Mike Miner; Susan L. Gordon, archivist, Tennessee State Library and Archives; Joe Cataio, Moody Bible Institute Archives; the Filson Historical Society; Jim Helm and Roberta Fairburn of the Abraham Lincoln Presidential Library and Museum; staff of the Tennessee State Library and Archives, Patty Bancroft Roberts, and others.

Lastly many thanks to Joseph Anthony Pucci for his support.

INTRODUCTION

Chicagoans are no more likely than most Americans to treasure the locales of their past. Catherine O'Leary's notorious barn disappeared in the 1871 fire her cow allegedly started, and there has been no attempt to restore it. Ironically a school for future firemen is built on its site. Only one building survives from the 1893 World's Columbian Exposition, and nothing is left of the 1933–1934 Century of Progress exposition, except for Northerly Island. Bubbly Creek, however, survives as a relic of the stockyards but now is the site of an elegant housing project. It still bubbles, incidentally.

There are no remnants or monuments on the former site of Camp Douglas. Indeed by 1870, the remnants of this prison camp for Confederate soldiers had disappeared from the site, which was once located between Thirty-first and Thirty-third Streets on Cottage Grove Avenue next to the University of Chicago, the Illinois Central tracks, and near the Washington Park race track. Who wants to remember a prison camp that many say was almost as bad as the Confederate Andersonville Civil War prison? Unless one is a Chicago history buff, one can drive by the site and neither feel a twitch of grief for the young men who suffered and died there nor remember anything about the great Camp Douglas conspiracy. In an age of Guantanamo and Abu Grab, that is unfortunate.

Camp Douglas and Andersonville were cruel and hellish places. Thousands died of disease, malnutrition, and despair; however, the main problem in Civil War prison camps was incompetence with some corruption mixed in. America had no experience in coping with large numbers of war prisoners. Moreover, there was so much suffering and death, that the prisoners seemed to be less than human to many of the camp personnel.

As it was reported in history books until almost the end of the 20th century, the great conspiracy was a dastardly plot to storm Camp Douglas and free the Confederate prisoners. The conspiracy was lead by copperheads (Confederate sympathizers) from Chicago, a team of Southern spies who were smuggled in from Canada, butternuts (so-called because of the color of their homespun Confederate uniforms), and downstate Illinois farmers who liked neither Pres. Abraham Lincoln nor his war. Downstate farmers were often sympathetic to the Southern cause because, culturally and religiously, they had more in common with those across the Ohio River than with those in the big cities further north. In Ohio, they were called Buckeyes, in Indiana they were called Hoosiers, and in Iowa they were known as Hawkeyes.

The unlikely scenario that sick and hungry prisoners were capable of making war was extremely improbable. Lincoln laughed when he was told about the conspiracy. In fact, less than 20 butternuts got north of Springfield and then turned back towards home. The guards at

Camp Douglas put down a bit of disorder among prisoners, and the spies were quickly picked up by Chicago police. Local Democrats were arrested and accused of being copperheads. Agitation for a peace conference to end the war was prima facie evidence of being a copperhead. Most of the accused men were acquitted in a military trial in Cincinnati, and the others were paroled or pardoned after the war. Some of them, however, died of the smallpox epidemic that was raging in Chicago at the time.

The conspiracy was then, at best, a fantasy of a handful of men who had no intention of burning down the city, much less marching to Rockford. However, William "Deacon" Bross, an editor for the *Chicago Tribune*, created a panic in the city with the myth of the great conspiracy. He solidified his version of the story in a lecture 10 years later to the Chicago Historical Society.

Historians and storytellers, in search of mystery and horror, courage and incompetence, love and hate, can still find much to explore in places like Camp Douglas and Chicago. If nothing else, they provide raw material for cautionary tales about dehumanizing prisoners.

—Andrew M. Greeley

One

CHICAGO ON THE EVE OF WAR

As Chicago entered the decade of the Civil War, it shed its image as a fur-trading frontier town. No longer a prairie outpost where residents hunted bear and lived in the rugged log cabins they built by hand, by 1860, Chicago hosted the presidential convention where future president Abraham Lincoln won the nomination of the Republican Party and formed an alliance of local business owners that controlled (and still control) the world's grain supply and eradicated the source of a deadly disease, among other accomplishments.

In 1860, Chicago's 110,000 residents enjoyed a lifestyle to rival that of European capitals. Newly-laid sidewalks kept clothing free of goopy mud that cursed earlier generations of fashion-conscious gentlemen and ladies and bred cholera that killed 5 percent of the city's population. A shopping spree in luxurious stores on Lake Street might include a stop at Park's for a ladies' party fan from Paris, a silk garter or a hairbrush made of real tortoise shell, then a look at hoop skirts at A. G. Downs and Company. There were, of course, no blues or jazz clubs in Chicago in 1860, but the abundance of nightlife choices included, for 25¢ per person, a performance by Mrs. Farren and her daughter Fanny Fitz Farren at the McVicker's Theatre; a memorial celebration of the life of Robert Burns; ball and banquet at the Briggs House; and at $3 per couple, a lecture by Ralph Waldo Emerson at Metropolitan Hall.

Chicago's prewar economy attracted visionary entrepreneurs determined to live a better life made even better by a steady cash flow. From Cleveland came Joseph Medill, who bought the fledging *Chicago Tribune*, which supported presidential candidate Abraham Lincoln. Lincoln's opponent, a Vermont farm boy named Stephen A. Douglas, amassed his fortune by selling his pricey real estate to the Illinois Central Railroad.

Preparing for a long life with his second wife and two young sons, Douglas planned to build a permanent home on Chicago's South Side. Little did he know that, within one year, he would die in a hotel room and his cherished land would become the site of the deadliest prison in American history.

Stephen A. Douglas Archrival of Abraham Lincoln. Vermont native Stephen A. Douglas moved to Illinois where he served as a United States senator from 1847 until his death. Douglas opposed federal legislation to build a transcontinental railroad across the South and promoted a northern route with its hub in Chicago, where Douglas owned property. Standing at just over five feet tall, he debated six-foot-five-inch Abraham Lincoln and earned the name, "the Little Giant," for his persuasive political powers. After Douglas's wife died in childbirth, he married a woman half his age. Adele Cutts, Dolley Madison's great-niece, quickly adjusted to life as stepmother of Douglas's two sons, Robert and Stephen, but Douglas's plan to build a family home on Chicago's South Side was cut short with his death from typhoid fever at the Tremont House Hotel on June 3, 1861. (Left, courtesy of the Chicago History Museum; below, courtesy of the Library of Congress.)

ABRAHAM LINCOLN. As young men with strong but opposing beliefs, Lincoln and Douglas often crossed paths. The pair exchanged political views in the back of Joshua Speed's store in Springfield, and in 1840, after Lincoln broke his engagement to Kentucky belle Mary Todd, Douglas courted Lincoln's future wife. Lincoln challenged incumbent Douglas in the 1858 United States senate race, suggesting a series of debates across Illinois. Initially declined by Douglas, who ultimately won reelection, the debates brought Lincoln to national prominence and aided in his nomination as the Republican Party's presidential candidate at the Wigwam in Chicago in 1860. Lincoln's Democratic opponent was Douglas, who was a loyal supporter of the Union. After the attack on Fort Sumter, Douglas suggested to Lincoln that he, Douglas, undertake a speaking tour of the western states and border states to rally support for the president. It was while taking a break during this speaking tour that Douglas died in Chicago. (Courtesy of the Library of Congress.)

UNIVERSITY OF CHICAGO. The University of Chicago's long history and its luminaries are well known, but before John D. Rockefeller, Enrico Fermi, and Milton Friedman, there was Sen. Stephen A. Douglas. Douglas donated 10 acres of land on Chicago's South Side to an organization of Baptists to establish a new university. Local newspapers criticized the senator's motives as less than altruistic. The donated land was appraised at $50,000, but with a university on his land, the value of Douglas's estate surrounding the campus increased substantially. The *Chicago Tribune* claimed he bound the trustees "strongly to certain conditions, among which were the making of specified costly improvements, which cannot be made without enhancing his adjoining acres. . . . [It was] a bargain by which he will put $10,000 to $20,000 in his pocket." A crowd of 4,000 attended the laying of the cornerstone ceremony on July 4, 1857. (Courtesy of the Chicago Public Library.)

MCVICKER'S THEATRE AND JOHN
WILKES BOOTH. As the prospect of war
loomed, Chicagoans sought comfort in
local entertainment palaces such as Rice's
Theater. Opera became a popular diversion
when introduced in 1850; however, a fire
that consumed the theater during the
premiere of *La Sonnambula* ended Chicago's
first opera season. Eager for a replacement,
Marshall Field and Potter Palmer supported
actor James McVicker's bid to open the
palatial McVicker's Theatre, where the
nation's prominent stage actors appeared,
including the famous Booth family. James
McVicker's daughter Mary became John
Wilkes Booth's sister-in-law when she
married his brother Edwin, who was shot
at during a performance at the McVicker's
Theatre. Actor and assassin John Wilkes
Booth appeared in the theater's 1862
performance of *Richard III*. (Above,
Courtesy of the Chicago Public Library.)

CURIOSITIES. For hard-working citizens who enjoyed less haughty entertainment, Chicago offered a peek at the weird, the unusual, and the freaky. A Dearborn Street venue exhibited live curiosities including a man reputed to be one foot taller than Mayor "Long John" Wentworth, conjoined twins, and a Cuban snake. Kingsbury Hall on Randolph Street, known for art and classical music, changed hands during the Civil War and reopened with exhibits from P. T. Barnum's bankrupt New York museum. Reopened as Colonel Wood's Museum and Gallery of Nature and Art, shown above in 1865, the venue delighted Civil War–era crowds with an array of 200,000 oddities including the Invisible Lady, the Smallest Lady in the World, and "Old Neptune, The Sea Lion." (Courtesy of the Chicago Public Library.)

"LONG JOHN" WENTWORTH. A two-time Chicago mayor from 1857 to 1858 and 1860 to 1861, the 300-pound, six-foot-six-inch Wentworth was a force to be reckoned with. After a disgruntled citizen battered him with a hickory cane until it snapped, the mayor simply refreshed himself with a splash of cold water at the Tremont House Hotel. On another occasion at the Tremont, Wentworth introduced the Chicago press corps to the Prince of Wales saying, "Boys, this is the prince. Prince, these are the boys." As a U.S. congressman, Wentworth supported the federal land grant that benefited Stephen A. Douglas's purchase of the site of the future Camp Douglas. Wentworth also carried Abraham Lincoln's coffin when the presidential funeral train stopped in Chicago. (Right, Courtesy of the Chicago Public Library.)

SHOPPING ALONG LAKE STREET. In the 1860s, Chicago newspapers filled their pages with advertisements from Lake Street stores offering a bewildering array of goods. J. A. Smith and Company at 118 Lake Street advertised 1,500 buffalo robes. Penton and Company sold cough drops at 55¢ per box with a guarantee that the lozenges did not "contain opium or anything injurious." Barnum Brothers at 138 Lake Street played it safe by offering both "Lincoln and Hamlin" and "Douglas and Johnson" presidential campaign badges. Chicago's swampy land posed problems to fashion-conscious shoppers, and when Chicago leaders determined that raising streets and buildings would result in less mud on its citizens' shoes and the elimination of cholera, the engineering feat was immortalized in a lithograph produced by Edward Mendel of 162 Lake Street. (Courtesy of the Chicago Public Library.)

TREMONT HOUSE HOTEL. After burning to the ground twice, Ira Couch rebuilt his Tremont House Hotel for $75,000. A favorite of young attorney Abraham Lincoln, the Tremont saw its share of significant historical events, including Stephen A. Douglas's death from typhoid fever. In 1858, Douglas spoke to supporters from the hotel balcony as did Abraham Lincoln the following evening. In 1859, exotically dressed Camp Douglas guards performed military drills at the hotel. The Republican National Convention of 1860 delegates stayed at the Tremont while considering presidential candidates. After Lincoln's assassination, the first lady and her two sons stayed at the Tremont and, later, Robert Todd Lincoln became a regular tenant. The Tremont relocated to its current site in 1939. (Courtesy of the Chicago Public Library.)

190.—*River Scene, looking South from Madison St. Bridge.*

CHICAGO RIVER. In the years preceding the Civil War, coal, salt, flour, barley, and wool arrived in Chicago via the busy Chicago River along with cholera, typhoid, animal carcasses, and human waste. An epidemic of cholera killed 6 percent of the population in 1854, and death from typhoid fever averaged 65 per 100,000 Chicagoans. City officials hired Ellis Sylvester Chesbrough, a Boston engineer, to modernize Chicago's water supply and sewage system. Using dredged soil from the Chicago River, Chesbrough recommended raising the downtown buildings the height of Mayor "Long John" Wentworth. Chesbrough continued working on city projects during the Civil War and was called upon to inspect sanitary conditions at Camp Douglas. (Courtesy of the Chicago Public Library.)

52.—Sherman House.

THE SHERMAN HOUSE HOTEL. Owned by bricklayer and Chicago mayor Francis C. Sherman and considered the finest hotel in America, the hotel housed Camp Douglas officials. The officials preferred the hotel's luxurious amenities, including a gentlemen's conversation parlor and hot cupboards for keeping dinner plates warm, over the muddy and unsanitary prison camp. Even Union army horses preferred to board at the Sherman House Hotel. The *Chicago Tribune* reported that crowds gathered at the hotel stables to witness the selection of horses "brought up for enlistment into the U.S. Army," and determined the purchase of 2,000 horses at $110 each brought a "handsome sum" of $200,000 to Chicago. When the Douglas brigade departed for St. Louis, they paraded past the hotel where "handkerchiefs fluttered from windows like doves." (Courtesy of the Chicago Public Library.)

ILLINOIS CENTRAL RAILROAD. Railroads, including the Illinois Central Railroad, transformed Chicago from a small town to a vital transportation center, transporting grain, lumber, and an endless supply of coal from downstate Illinois to feed the furnaces of factories. During the Civil War, the government appropriated the Illinois Central Railroad to bring Confederate prisoners to Camp Douglas and inadvertently provided an escape route. By walking along railroad tracks that ran a few hundreds yards from Camp Douglas's east entrance, prisoners found their way to downtown Chicago, where they blended into the population. After Camp Douglas closed, some officials argued to keep the Camp Douglas station open, but it was torn down with the rest of the camp. (Courtesy of the Chicago Public Library.)

THE ILLINOIS CENTRAL RAILROAD STATION, 1856.

ONE OF THE SIXTEEN HISTORICAL PAINTINGS BY LAWRENCE C. EARLE IN THE BANKING ROOM OF THE CENTRAL TRUST COMPANY OF ILLINOIS . 152 MONROE ST. CHICAGO.

THE SALOON BUILDING. Built in 1836 at Lake Street and Clark Street, the saloon was not a saloon as one would think. Derived from the French word "salon," The Saloon Building offered space for "public entertainment of various kinds, political and religious meetings, concerts, traveling shows, etc.," according to A. T. Andreas's *History of Chicago.* Here Chicagoans approved the city's 1837 charter. The ground floor held several small shops where Chicagoans purchased goods such as perfumes, paints, and pharmaceuticals sold by F. Scammon. The Saloon Building also housed Chicago's first city hall from 1837 to 1842 and the United States Circuit Court where Abraham Lincoln argued cases before federal judges, including cases on behalf of the Illinois Central Railroad. A new courthouse (below) was built to replace these facilities. (Courtesy of the Chicago Public Library.)

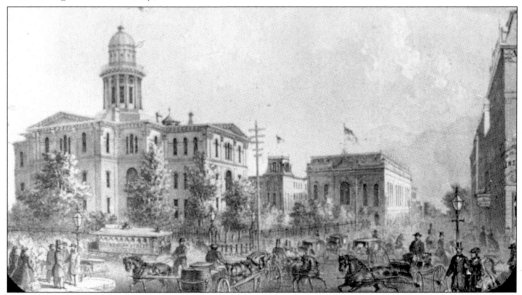

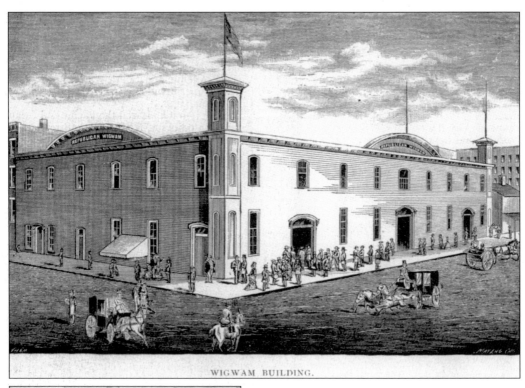

WIGWAM BUILDING.

WIGWAM BUILDING. Hastily built at Lake Street and Market Street (now Wacker Drive) for $5,000 to house the Republication Convention, it earned the unofficial name, "the Wigwam," which was a derogatory term for poorly-constructed buildings. In 1860, delegates to the Republican National Convention favored New York senator William H. Seward for the presidential nomination, but with the support of powerful newspaper editor Joseph Medill, Abraham Lincoln won the nomination. During the Democratic National Convention of 1864, also held at the Wigwam, a conspiracy to disrupt the convention and release Camp Douglas prisoners was hatched, causing a delay of the start of the convention from July to August and the declaration of martial law to protect Chicago's citizens from roving bands of Confederate soldiers. (Courtesy of the Chicago Public Library.)

DR. NATHAN SMITH DAVIS. Prior to arriving in Chicago to accept a position at Rush Medical College, this 30-year-old New York physician founded the American Medical Association. While in Chicago, he advocated the abolition of slavery, spoke at Stephen A. Douglas's funeral, and opposed legislation proposed by Lincoln (below) to establish a homeopathic college in Chicago, a move Davis considered a threat to the American Medical Association. Well regarded as a physician, he drew the ire of the local government when he brought public attention to preventable diseases and the lack of public health officials. Although Davis's contributions to improving Chicago's public health may be forgotten, astute Evanstonians are aware that Davis Street is named for his role in founding what is now the medical school at Northwestern University. (Right, courtesy of *Bygone Days in Chicago.*)

THOMAS B. BRYAN. Although he lost his bid to become mayor of Chicago, this Harvard-trained lawyer spent his fortune to provide Chicagoans with first-class amenities. One of his early projects was to purchase land along Green Bay Road, now Clark Street, and hire landscape architect H. W. S. Cleveland to design Graceland Cemetery. He brought culture to Chicago. At Bryan Hall, Chicagoans marveled at paintings such as *Franklin at the Court of France*, listened to opera, and attended charitable functions. He served as president of the YMCA and provided the organization with meeting rooms and a library. He collected money for the care of Union soldiers from all states and served as president of the Old Soldiers' Home near Camp Douglas. At an auction to raise money for the Union cause, he purchased a copy of the Emancipation Proclamation signed by Pres. Abraham Lincoln, which he donated to the Old Soldiers' Home. Unfortunately, the document perished in the Chicago Fire of 1871. (Courtesy of *Bygone Days in Chicago*.)

ST. JAMES EPISCOPAL CHURCH. Rev. Robert Clarkson, pastor of St. James Episcopal Church, strongly supported parishioners called to defend the Union cause. A practical man, he composed a prayer for soldiers that includes the words, "keep me from the vices of a soldier's calling." In May 1861, he conducted a religious service for members of the Sturgis Rifles training near the University of Chicago on Cottage Grove Avenue, and he delivered sermons at the funerals of Brig. Gen. T. E. G. Ransom and Col. Elmer Ephraim Ellsworth, early war casualties. Although the Chicago Fire of 1871 destroyed most of St. James church, a section containing a memorial to its Civil War heroes was only blackened by smoke. (Above, courtesy of the Chicago Public Library; right, courtesy of *Bygone Days in Chicago*.)

MARY LIVERMORE. Bostonian Mary Ashton Rice Livermore arrived in Chicago as a preacher's wife, but her commitment to helping those less fortunate extended beyond her husband's church. She helped found the Chicago Home for Aged Women and the Hospital for Women and Children. During Chicago's Republican National Convention of 1860, she reported on the nomination of Abraham Lincoln for a Christian newspaper. Livermore inspected sanitary conditions at Camp Douglas and, during the Civil War, she organized a fair in Chicago to raise money to purchase clothing and equipment for Union soldiers. Thinking big, she appealed to Lincoln for a donation and, with his contribution of a signed, handwritten copy of the Emancipation Proclamation, the Northwestern Sanitary Commission raised $100,000. (Left, courtesy of the Chicago Public Library; below, courtesy of the Chicago History Museum.)

Two

CONFEDERATE PRISONERS ARRIVE IN CHICAGO

Newspaper accounts of the day painted a rosy picture of conditions at Camp Douglas. The *Chicago Tribune* reported that, in choosing the location of the Union army training camp, "the most careful reference was paid to the great leading features of the ease of access, nature of site, extent of area and abundant supply of water. . . . The water to the camp will be supplied direct from city hydrants on the grounds. The City Railway Company [an early mass transit system] are to carry, free, officers and soldiers in the business of the camp." In the fall of 1861, more than 3,500 soldiers filled newly-constructed barracks at Camp Douglas, drilling daily under the command of Col. Joseph Tucker. The mood was light on one evening in December, when soldiers washed windows and strung paper lanterns around the camp in preparation for an official dance attended by ladies from Chicago. By February of the following year, rumors swirled around Chicago that Camp Douglas would receive thousands of Confederate prisoners. The *Chicago Tribune* dismissed the idea of keeping prisoners at Camp Douglas, "where the strongest guard couldn't keep in a drunken corporal, is rich." Within a few weeks, Camp Douglas received 5,500 Confederate prisoners captured at Fort Donelson. When the prisoners arrived, the *Chicago Tribune* claimed that prisoners received "the identical accommodations and the same fare as were recently according to our own troops," and rations "being equal to the bet anywhere issued." For a time, Confederate prisoners moved freely among Union trainees awaiting orders to ship out. Curious Chicago civilians rode horse-drawn streetcars along Cottage Grove Avenue to the gates of Camp Douglas, where they ate picnic lunches and gawked at Confederate prisoners. The mood turned deadly at Camp Douglas after Civil War battles resulted in high casualties of Union troops.

FIRST UNION ARMY CASUALTY. Elmer Ephraim Ellsworth, a Chicago law clerk, is widely recognized as the first Union army casualty of the Civil War. Ellsworth's crack drill team, known as Zouaves, gained fame at the National Agricultural Society Fair in September 1859 that was held on the muddy grounds that later became Camp Douglas. As Ellsworth's Zouaves departed for a 20-city tour, thousands of Chicagoans gathered to bid the group farewell. Shot while pulling down a Confederate flag in Virginia, his body was brought to the White House where Pres. Abraham Lincoln exclaimed, "My boy! My boy! Was it necessary this sacrifice should be!" Oddly the Confederate flag that cost Ellsworth his life became a favorite plaything of Tad Lincoln, who enjoyed waving it from White House windows. (Left, courtesy of Chicago Public Library; below, courtesy of the Library of Congress.)

Gunboat anchored opposite Cairo 1864.

PRISONERS ARRIVE IN CHICAGO. An early Union victory resulted in an unexpected dilemma of caring for prisoners of war for Gen. Ulysses S. Grant. What should be done with thousands of prisoners of war? How much would it cost to feed them? Where would they go? Chicago would seem an unlikely place for a Confederate prison camp, but with little advance notice, Gen. Allen C. Fuller ordered Camp Douglas to accept thousands of prisoners captured at Fort Donelson and, by early March 1862, approximately 5,500 prisoners poured into Chicago. They came to the city from the battlefield by train, on foot, and aboard riverboats. A few of the boats caught fire en route from southern Illinois, and Confederate soldiers were shot at by angry civilians hiding along riverbanks. (Courtesy of the Chicago History Museum.)

CHURCH AND STATE. Local religious leaders who preached sermons in a small chapel at Camp Douglas worked diligently to spread their brand of religion among Confederate prisoners. Occasionally people from out of town, such as Parson William Gannaway Brownlow of Tennessee, drew large crowds at Camp Douglas, but Brownlow's fellow Southerners did not necessarily agree with his message, which was a mixture of religion and politics. This Methodist preacher and former slaveholder had fled the South and booked himself on a tour of northern states after his imprisonment for publishing pro-Union articles in *Brownlow's Whig*, the newspaper he edited. After the Civil War, Brownlow was elected governor of Tennessee, replacing his rival Andrew Johnson. One of Brownlow's early acts as governor was to trade Tennessee's cache of gold for United States bonds. In retaliation for Cave Johnson's surrender of Clarksville to the Union, he refused to seat Cave as a state senator. (Courtesy of the Chicago History Museum.)

GEORGE F. ROOT. Some of the most patriotic Civil War songs were composed and published in a Chicago store at 95 Clark Street. Stirring lyrics from "Just Before the battle, Mother," and "Tramp, Tramp, Tramp," were written by George F. Root, co-owner of the Root and Cady Music Store, a man who never served in battle. In addition to publishing and selling sheet music, Root and Cady brokered tickets to everything from classical music concerts to a performance by monkeys, dogs, and goats at Metropolitan Hall. When some prosperous ladies from Chicago decided to collect food for Union soldiers at Camp Douglas, the music store served as a repository for donations of chickens, parsnips, tea, sugar, coffee, pickles, and other food items. (Courtesy of *Bygone Days in Chicago*.)

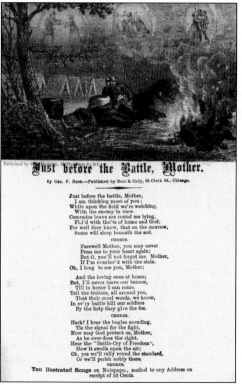

SOLDIERS FILL DOWNTOWN CHICAGO. By May 1861, Chicago's volunteer army reached 4,700 men, and the sight of Union army soldiers was not unusual to businessmen who worked in Chicago's busy commercial district or to women shopping on Lake Street. The *Chicago Tribune* reported that "men in uniform meet the eye at every street corner throughout the day." Col. Elmer Ephraim Ellsworth's Zouaves, who later guarded Confederate prisoners at Camp Douglas, presented exhibition drills outside the Tremont House Hotel, and some errant soldiers who were bored waiting for battle spent their time in Chicago taverns and brothels. Because Illinois governor Richard Yates's selection of regiments included only soldiers from downstate and none from Chicago, prominent citizens appealed to the governor to accept local volunteers. As men marched to downtown railway stations to board trains for the battlefield, they were greeted by crowds of cheering Chicagoans. (Courtesy of the Chicago History Museum.)

DR. WILLIAM W. EVERTS. Dr. William W. Everts, a Baptist minister who left Kentucky because of his antislavery views, arrived in Chicago as pastor of the First Baptist Church and soon retired the church debt. While he raised funds for the church, his wife solicited donations of bibles for Camp Douglas soldiers and joined the sanitary commission's efforts to raise funds. (Courtesy of the Chicago Public Library.)

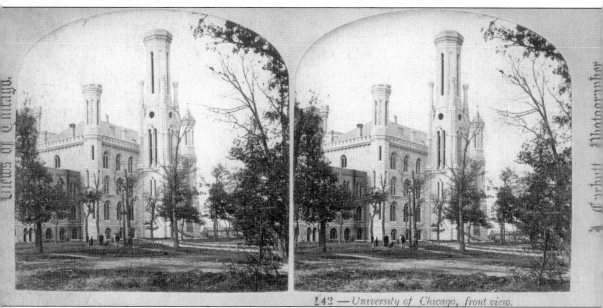

142 — University of Chicago, front view.

UNIVERSITY OF CHICAGO. The entire Everts family raised money for the continued operation of the University of Chicago that was situated on Stephen A. Douglas's land. Despite their extraordinary efforts, however, they could not save the university when enrollment declined because of problems with its neighbor, Camp Douglas. (Courtesy of *Bygone Days in Chicago*.)

154—Interior Grace Church Wabash Ave.

GRACE CHURCH. With generous financial support from devout churchgoers, towering stone churches appeared in the Chicago skyline, replacing wooden cabins built in the 1830s. Among them was Grace church, shown here in the late 1860s. During the Civil War, the generosity of Grace Church members was not confined to simply building the magnificent church. On December 18, 1861, ladies of Grace Church formed the Camp Douglas Hospital Aid Society. With permission from Col. Benjamin J. Sweet, commander of Camp Douglas, female members of Grace Church provided medical assistance to prisoners confined to the prison's hospital, and in 1863, the women opened a store on State Street that provided work for wives of Union soldiers. In 1864, Grace Church members established St. Luke's Hospital, which continues as part of Rush Medical Center on Chicago's Near West Side. Members of other Chicago churches preached Sunday sermons at Camp Douglas and baptized hundreds of Confederate prisoners. (Courtesy of the Chicago Public Library.)

MAYOR JULIAN S. RUMSEY. Upon the death of Stephen A. Douglas, Mayor Julian S. Rumsey called for the closure of all Chicago businesses for a day of citywide mourning. At a cost of $1,754.64 to Chicago taxpayers, he also called for the city coffers to pay for Douglas's funeral. A strong supporter of the Union while serving as president of the Chicago Board of Trade, Rumsey had no desire to hold elected office when friends nominated him to be mayor, but when he was elected in April 1861, he promised to serve the citizens of Chicago to the best of his abilities. As a preventive measure, Rumsey ordered 500 muskets to be sent to Chicago from Springfield to protect Chicagoans at the start of the Civil War. The mayor offered the Chicago Board of Trade's meeting rooms to new recruits, and to show their gratitude, a group of volunteer soldiers dubbed themselves the Rumsey Rifle Guard. (Courtesy of the Chicago Public Library.)

TENNESSEE SOLDIERS AT CAMP DOUGLAS. These infantrymen from the 48th Tennessee Infantry arrived at Camp Douglas after their defeat at Fort Donelson. As was the custom, the victor of a battle sent officers and enlisted men to separate prisons to prevent them from organizing a revolt. While these enlisted men were incarcerated in Chicago's Camp Douglas, their commanding officers spent time at Fort Warren in Massachusetts and Johnson's Island on Lake Erie. During Pvt. Anderson Churchwell's incarceration at Camp Douglas, the Union army used his family's Tennessee farm to feed troops. The wife of this 41-year-old soldier and farmer became incensed as Union soldiers used the farm's fences for firewood, and she reprimanded the commanding officer for his actions. The couple's son Jonathan, who tended the farm with his mother, followed in his father's footsteps after the incident and both men returned to Tennessee after the Civil War.

HENRY MORTON STANLEY. Years before he uttered the famous phrase, "Dr. Livingston, I presume," African explorer and British journalist Henry Morton Stanley (whose real name was John Rowlands) claimed he was captured at the Battle of Shiloh as a member of the 6th Arkansas Infantry Regiment and held prisoner at Camp Douglas. While most historians believe that, as a teenager, Stanley worked his way to America as a cabin boy aboard a commercial ship and that he fought at the Battle of Shiloh, some question the validity of his claim that he was ever held prisoner or even visited Camp Douglas. The military's poorly-kept records do not list a Henry Morton Stanley or a John Rowlands, yet in published accounts of his stay at Camp Douglas, he provides remarkably specific details of life as a prisoner of war.

JOHN L. HANCOCK. As a meatpacking mogul and future president of the Chicago Board of Trade, John L. Hancock raised money to establish and support Illinois troops, promising $100 upon signing, $13 to $20 per month, and $75 at the end of the war. He presided over the formation of the Chicago Board of Trade battery, which fought seven battles. This battery of 156 men was sworn in on August 2, 1862, and feted with a reception at the Chicago Board of Trade. In other duties, he judged target practice by Zouaves and presented a silver medal to the best shot. Camp Hancock, located a few hundred yards south of Camp Douglas, and the Hancock Guard, Company A of the Board of Trade Regiment, were named in his honor. He died in 1890 and was buried at Oak Woods Cemetery near the Confederate Mound. (Courtesy of *Bygone Days in Chicago*.)

GOV. RICHARD YATES. On April 16, 1861, Illinois governor Richard Yates issued a proclamation to convene the general assembly for the purpose of calling for troops and raising financial support for the war. Assuming that the war would be over in a matter of weeks, the state legislature authorized the enlistment of 125 officers and 4,458 soldiers, including musicians, wagoners, and surgeons for three months of service. Seeing a need for more military training camps, Yates declared 25 counties surrounding Chicago as the Northern Military District of Illinois and Camp Douglas as the district's official training center. The financial support promised by Yates included outfitting Illinois soldiers for battle. Upon arriving at Camp Douglas, each soldier was issued a knapsack, canteen, bayonet, scabbard, blankets, half a tent (his roommate carried the other half), a uniform, several pairs of wool socks, and flannel underwear. By 1865, Illinois' commitment grew to more than 250,000.

JOSEPH MEDILL. Canadian Joseph Medill praised Pres. Abraham Lincoln in his newspaper, the *Chicago Tribune,* and challenged Stephen A. Douglas to accept Lincoln's invitation to debate, writing that if Douglas refused, "it will be because he is a coward." Although Medill supported the war, he angered the president by complaining about Illinois' contribution. Lincoln reprimanded him saying, "after Boston, Chicago has been the chief instrument in bringing this war on the country. . . . It is you who are largely responsible for making blood flow as it has. You called for war until we had it. . . . Now you come here begging to be let off from the call for men. . . . You ought to be ashamed." (Courtesy of the Chicago Public Library.)

JOSEPH MEDILL'S GRAVE. Through tenacious investigating, Medill's staff uncovered hundreds of deaths not officially reported at Camp Douglas. (Author's collection.)

CARTE DE VISITE. Daniel F. Brandon, a local Chicago photographer, made a tidy income running the Camp Douglas photograph studio where he churned out portraits of Union guards and Confederate prisoners. As was the fashion, Brandon mounted prints onto small presentation cards. The so-called carte de visite or CDV could be presented in person on a social visit or mailed to family members at home. To finance the Civil War in its later years, the federal government raised taxes and imposed a new tax on an odd assortment of items, including legal documents, playing cards, and patent medicines. From 1864 through 1866, federal law required a 2¢ revenue stamp to be affixed to the reverse side of "photographs, daguerreotypes or any other sun-pictures," including CDVs. After the closure of Camp Douglas, Brandon opened a studio in downtown Chicago, but the Chicago Fire of 1871 destroyed the studio and most of his Camp Douglas photographs. (Courtesy of the Chicago Public Library.)

FORT DONELSON. Fighting together with their Northern brothers, 30 Illinois regiments shared in the North's first major victory. Chicago joyfully greeted the unconditional surrender of the Confederate army at Fort Donelson with a day of citywide celebrations. Shops closed and thousands of citizens gathered in the streets to dance and cheer. Couriers quickly carried the news to Union soldiers training at Camp Douglas. According to the *Chicago Tribune*, "the announcement was made to the soldiers and received with the wildest enthusiasm. The entire camp was in a blaze with excitement. The camp cannon, guns, pistols and everything that could make noise was called into requisition." Within a few days, 5,500 Confederate prisoners arrived at Camp Douglas, where they joined Union troops from the Irish Brigade, Colonel Voss's Cavalry Regiment, Bouton's Battery, Bolton's Battery, and the 51st Illinois Regiment. (Courtesy of the Chicago History Museum.)

MAYOR FRANCIS SHERMAN. Shortly after Confederate prisoners poured into Camp Douglas, Mayor Francis Sherman (right) and Col. James A. Mulligan (below) took a secret train ride to Springfield at the request of Gov. Richard Yates, who was ordered by the secretary of war to send all Camp Douglas guards into battle. Upon his return to Chicago the next day, Sherman hastily called a public meeting at Metropolitan Hall to raise two regiments of soldiers to serve as Camp Douglas guards for three months. The crowd waited for adjunct general Allen C. Fuller, and by the time the meeting got underway, the general called for the organization of three regiments, one of which would begin guard duty the following morning. The editor of *Chicago Tribune* supported the call for volunteers saying, "Let every man, high or low in station, who can leave his business and shoulder a musket, come up immediately." Sherman served as mayor of Chicago from April 1862 to April 1865. (Right, courtesy of the Chicago Public Library; below, courtesy of *Bygone Days in Chicago*.)

TRINITY CHURCH. On a cold Sunday afternoon, in February 1862, more than 500 members of the 57th Regiment of Illinois Volunteers marched three miles from Camp Douglas to Trinity church for a special service prior to marking their departure for battle against the Confederates. A combination of patriotic and religious rites, the church organ played "The Star Spangled Banner," a heavenly choir sang "America," and Rev. James Pratt preached the duty of men to God and country. Later that month, Pratt journeyed from Trinity church to Camp Douglas, where he preached to Confederate prisoners captured at Fort Donelson, saying, "I do not ask whether you came from the North or the South. You are immortal men . . . believe in the Lord Jesus Christ, and you will be saved." At the conclusion of his sermon, Pratt distributed religious pamphlets to hundreds of grateful prisoners. (Courtesy of the Chicago Public Library.)

HENRY GRAVES'S COTTAGE ON COTTAGE GROVE AVENUE. Henry Graves and his family refused to give up their land off Cottage Grove Avenue to make room for Camp Douglas, so the federal government built the Camp Douglas fence around the property that included 30 acres of land and the Graves family home. The Graves family occupied their house while thousands of Confederate prisoners lived on the other side of the fence. Although Graves and his family have since been forgotten, Chicagoans and ghost hunters may recognize *Eternal Silence* by Lorado Taft, the scary, hooded statue sculpted in Graceland Cemetery that marks the grave of Dexter Graves, the father of Henry. (Courtesy of the Chicago Public Library.)

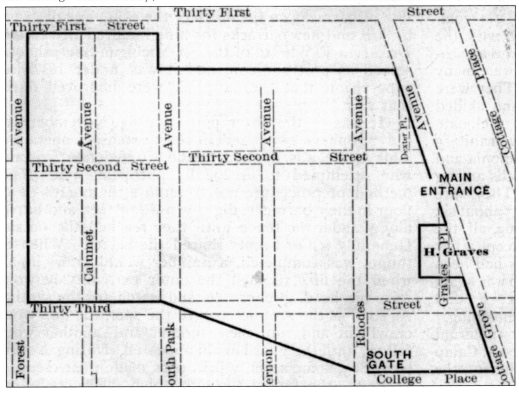

SAUVE ZOUAVE. Among the more colorful soldiers during the Civil War were the Zouaves, whose uniform consisted of baggy, red pants, white leggings, a red-trimmed jacket, and a red fez with a golden tassel. These men took their name and mode of dress from a highly-skilled French military unit composed of Algerian soldiers called Zouaoua. Four Chicago members of Col. Elmer Ephraim Ellsworth's Zouaves joined the New York Zouaves and fought at Richmond. Late in the Civil War, 600 Confederate prisoners took the oath of allegiance to the Union government under the direction of Ellsworth's Zouaves and joined the United States naval service. Despite the death of Ellsworth, their founder, early in the war, the Illinois regiment drilled relentlessly including at public performances in Waukegan and Du Page County. In May 1862, Ellsworth's Zouaves guarded Camp Douglas. (Courtesy of *Bygone Days in Chicago*.)

MUSIC AT CAMP DOUGLAS. Because music enhanced military morale and musical instruments posed no security threat, Union guards allowed music to ring throughout Camp Douglas. Small ensembles earned extra food, and a group of African American Confederate soldiers who organized a minstrel show played to sell-out crowds, earning more than just their salary as Confederate soldiers. One homesick prisoner, Joseph Dunavan of Company D, 2nd Regiment, Kentucky Cavalry, spent his free time as a composer. One of his songs, "Twas a Pleasant Home of Ours, Sister," is still sold and sung today. It is marketed through online auctions and distributed at Civil War reenactments. Neatly written with great care on paper he procured at Camp Douglas, the melancholy song begins with the words, "Twas a pleasant home of ours sister, In the summertime of our life." (Right, courtesy of the Chicago History Museum; below, courtesy of the Tennessee State Library and Archive.)

CAMP NEWSPAPER. In March 1864, members of the 14th Kentucky Cavalry Regiment, Morgan's Raiders, published a four-page newspaper called the *Prisoner Vidette*. The name was derived from a variation on the Italian word for sentinel, and the handwritten newspaper carried reports and rumors. In addition to serious articles about unsanitary conditions and smallpox at Camp Douglas, prisoners placed personal advertisements, such as, "Wanted a Save Conductor out of Camp Douglas. Any price will be paid for the secret. Rebel," which was a sly reference to escape tunnels being dug by Morgan's Raiders. Pvt. Abraham Lappin, who spent two years as a prisoner of war, placed an advertisement for handmade smoking pipes, sold "wholesale and retail at Lappins factory. Block 17 three doors west of the south east corner. Give him a call you will not be otherwise than satisfied." (Courtesy of the Chicago Public Library.)

THE IRISH BRIGADE. Col. James A. Mulligan's rousing speech to Chicago's Irish immigrants in April 1861 resulted in 1,000 new recruits and large financial contributions from Chicago's leading citizens. After losing a battle in Missouri, the colonel and the Irish Brigade were assigned to Camp Douglas guard duty. Eager to return to battle, the men scuffled with prisoners and, at a Chicago beer garden, three inebriated members of the Irish Brigade allegedly stole a gold watch. Some Irish Brigade soldiers wounded in battle, such as Martin Scully, an immigrant from County Tipperary, returned to Chicago and held elected office; however, Mulligan did not return to Chicago alive. He was shot as he shouted, "Lay me down and save the flag!" When his body was brought back to Chicago, a committee of leading Chicagoans, including Thomas Hoyne, met at the Tremont House Hotel to plan his funeral. He was buried in Calvary Cemetery in suburban Evanston. (Courtesy of the Chicago Public Library.)

DR. CHARLES VOLNEY DYER. Facing a shortage of guards at Camp Douglas, the City of Chicago appealed to prominent citizens, including physician Charles V. Dyer, to form a new regiment to fill in as temporary guards. Formation of the Home Guards was hampered, however, by a lack of weapons. Dyer, a strong abolitionist, gave stirring speeches at political rallies sponsored by a faction of the Republication Party called, "the Wide-Awakes." For his work supporting the Union, Pres. Abraham Lincoln appointed Dyer as a judge of the court of claims under the slave trade treaty with Great Britain to end the African slave trade. Dyer continued to be active in local politics while commuting between Chicago and Sierra Leone where the court conducted its business. Dyer lived on State Street and maintained his medical practice on Lake Street until his death in 1878. (Courtesy of *Bygone Days in Chicago*.)

MOTIVATIONAL SPEAKER. As the war continued, the 196th Regiment of the Pennsylvania Infantry was sent to Chicago to guard Camp Douglas prisoners of war, arriving in August and departing in mid-November 1864. Organized just one month earlier, the regiment became overwhelmed by unsanitary conditions and the responsibility of guarding 7,500 prisoners. To inspire the Pennsylvania soldiers, Gen. Williams S. Rosecrans, a West Point graduate, addressed the troops. Perhaps he did not cite as a motivating example his overwhelming defeat at the battle of Chickamauga a few months earlier. In town that summer to give a speech to members of the Chicago Board of Trade, Rosecrans almost apologized for his presence in Chicago, "I came to this city by accident and had no intention of appearing before you. . . . If you keep it secret till ten o'clock tonight I will be out of your way."

Miss Ada E. Sweet.

GIRL WHO LIVED AT CAMP DOUGLAS. When Col. Benjamin J. Sweet of the 21st Wisconsin Volunteer Infantry arrived in Chicago to take command of Camp Douglas, his 12-year-old daughter Ada accompanied him; however, Sweet's wife and other children remained in Wisconsin. To protect his daughter's welfare, Sweet lived in downtown Chicago until Secretary of War Edwin M. Stanton ordered him to live on base with or without his daughter. They moved to Camp Douglas and, with the exception of some underage prisoners of war, Ada was the only child. As a teenager, Ada attended a Catholic school and, although her father restricted the admission of nuns for the purpose of tending to sick prisoners, he allowed nuns from Ada's school to bring food to prisoners in the camp's hospital. In 1869, Sweet was appointed United States pension agent and moved his family to Lombard, Illinois. Ada, then 16 years old, became his secretary. Upon his death, Ada replaced him, and after a train killed her mother, she raised her brothers and sister. (Courtesy of the Chicago History Museum.)

GEORGE BRINTON MCCLELLAN. In 1861, Gen. George B. McClellan, who is pictured here with his wife, Ellen, ordered the 23rd Regiment of the Illinois Infantry, or the Irish Brigade, to guard Camp Douglas during a prisoner exchange. Displeased with the general's slow performance on the battlefield, an impatient Pres. Abraham Lincoln had relieved McClellan of his command saying, "If General McClellan does not want to use the army, I would like to borrow it for a time." Their lives intertwined again when McClellan ran for president against incumbent Lincoln. Plagued with problems, most notably a conspiracy of attack upon Camp Douglas, the Democratic National Convention of 1864 in Chicago was delayed for more than one month, but in the end, it did not matter, as Lincoln won reelection. Aware of his own shortcomings, McClellan said, "I can only seek fervently the guidance of the Ruler of the Universe, and, relying on His all-powerful aid, do my best to restore Union and peace to a suffering people, and to establish and guard their liberties and rights."

SPREADING THE GOSPEL. Dwight Lyman Moody (left) left his uncle's Boston shoe store to seek a rosier future. In Chicago, young Moody earned $5,000 and, with his personal savings, he operated a Sunday school for indigent Chicagoans. When Camp Douglas opened, Moody distributed religious materials to Union recruits, preached to the 72nd Illinois Volunteer Regiment and, with YMCA leaders, built a chapel at Camp Douglas. With the arrival of Confederate prisoners, Moody and others fought to provide religious services to the prisoners of war. Furious when Col. James A. Mulligan closed the chapel, YMCA president John V. Farwell (below), appealed to Secretary of War Edwin M. Stanton. After the war, Moody founded what is now the Moody Bible Institute on Chicago's North Side. (Left, courtesy of the Moody Bible Institute Archives; below, courtesy of *Bygone Days in Chicago*.)

Three

DEATH AND DISEASE STALK CAMP DOUGLAS

The Union army recorded the names of 26,060 Confederate soldiers held prisoner at Camp Douglas during the Civil War; more than 6,000 of those prisoners incarcerated at Camp Douglas were buried on Chicago's South Side. These deaths were not caused by wounds inflicted in battle, but by conditions at the camp.

Camp Douglas commanders reduced rations in retaliation for prisoners' infractions of camp rules. A daily portion of less than three ounces of inferior meat per person resulted in prisoners eating diseased rats and at least one dog. Guards beat hungry prisoners who took bones from garbage barrels. When vegetables were eliminated from the prison diet, nearly 4,000 men contracted scurvy. Sympathetic Chicagoans who brought seeds and vegetables were arrested and tried by a military court.

Overcrowding and unsanitary conditions, such as open latrines, contaminated drinking water, and animal feces, caused thousands of deaths from cholera, diphtheria, dysentery, measles, pneumonia, smallpox, tuberculosis, and typhoid fever. After the Battle of Shiloh, barracks overflowed with prisoners, and new detainees were housed in horse stables at the camp.

Cruel and unusual punishment weakened men's spirits and bodies. Soldiers who broke the rules or witnessed fellow prisoners committing infractions were forced to sit naked in the snow for hours. Three soldiers were hung by their thumbs until they passed out. Others were forced to sit for hours atop a 15-foot sawhorse, their legs stretched by weights. Officers who forced one prisoner to drag around a 30-pound ball chained to his leg did not allow its removal while he was hospitalized with smallpox.

Guards shot and killed prisoners. One black prisoner was killed by guards upon arrival as his regiment filed into Camp Douglas. A sick prisoner, who attempted to escape, was brought back and killed because he could not stand. After the prisoners' water supply was cut off, a thirsty soldier was shot and killed for eating snow.

Even after death, the journey of 6,000 men was not over.

PRISONERS OF WAR. Well-dressed confederate soldiers such as Mr. Hide and these unidentified Tennessee soldiers would bear little resemblance to their photographs after their time in Camp Douglas. Unless they could afford to purchase contraband clothing, or if they were able-bodied (many were not due to injuries or disease) and agreed to earn clothing in exchange for repairing barracks or digging sanitation trenches, the clothing they wore upon arrival would have to last until they were released. Laundry and bathing were limited, but prisoners were expected to keep themselves and their clothing clean. Failure to pass inspection resulted in being stripped naked and scrubbed until the offender bled. In addition to poor hygiene, diseases such as smallpox or scurvy, which ate away the mouth and jaw, disfigured thousands of soldiers. (Left, courtesy of Patty Roberts Bancroft; below, courtesy of Mike Miner.)

THE WOMEN AT CAMP DOUGLAS. Women appeared at Camp Douglas either as visitors or as prisoners. Mary Morris, wife of former Chicago mayor Buckner S. Morris, who arrived at Camp Douglas with food for prisoners, was imprisoned at Camp Douglas for her acts of kindness. One unidentified Chicago woman who visited the prison camp captured the heart of a prisoner of war, who escorted her around the crowded grounds as fellow prisoners shouted "Make way for a lady." After inspecting conditions at Camp Douglas, Mary Livermore of the Northwestern Sanitary Commission reported that prisoners were unfed and poorly clothed. Among the thousands of prisoners who lived under these conditions were at least five women, who either disguised themselves as men or accompanied their husbands from the battlefield to prison. One mother brought her young son with her to Camp Douglas where they stayed for several months. (Courtesy of the Chicago History Museum.)

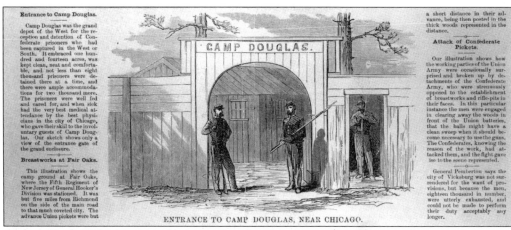

CAMP DOUGLAS.

ENTRANCE TO CAMP DOUGLAS, NEAR CHICAGO.

GUARD DUTY. The Union soldiers in this sketch appear relaxed, yet vigilant, as they guard the entrance to Camp Douglas. In reality, three guards with bayonets would not stand in the way of thousands of angry prisoners intent upon escaping. In fact, Camp Douglas guards were better-equipped and numbered in the hundreds. In 1863, while several units of guards were sent to battle, the remaining Camp Douglas guards were outfitted with six-shooter revolvers. One company of Union soldiers consisting of Chippewa and Ottawa Indians, who were armed with rifles and "shoot to kill" orders, patrolled barracks and grounds looking for likely suspects. But not all guards took their duties seriously. Some accepted substantial bribes from affluent prisoners looking for an easy way out. Others who went AWOL (absent without leave) were sent back to work by Chicago police officers paid to return guards they found in downtown brothels and taverns. (Courtesy of the Chicago History Museum.)

JOSEPH "FIGHTING JOE" HOOKER. Union army major general Joseph "Fighting Joe" Hooker, whose name is synonymous with the prostitutes who followed his troops, a practice he approved of to boost morale, delivered a speech at the Chicago Board of Trade interrupted by frequent cheers from the Chicago crowd.

GEN. JOSEPH HOOKER.
After lunching with some of
Chicago's most prosperous
traders, Gen. Joseph Hooker
took a carriage ride to Camp
Douglas where he gave high
praise to Camp Douglas
commander Col. Benjamin J.
Sweet and declared Camp
Douglas to be "the best prison
camp in the United States,"
according to the *Chicago
Tribune*. Hooker is buried
in Graceland Cemetery on
Chicago's North Side.

CHICAGO CITY RAILWAY COMPANY. Curious Chicagoans who wanted an up close and personal look at newly-captured Confederate prisoners of war could catch a horse-drawn wagon at the corner of State and Madison Streets for the three-mile journey to Cottage Grove Avenue and Thirty-first Street. Chicago's population included a number of affluent citizens who left the south to establish flourishing businesses in Chicago, but kept strong familial ties with the South. Some of these citizens brought food to the camp or departed Camp Douglas with a prisoner as guards looked the other way. However, any citizen with a few cents and a picnic lunch could enjoy a Sunday afternoon gawking at the enemy. To save paper, which was in short supply during the Civil War years, the Chicago City Railway Company printed multiple-ride punch tickets, which meant citizens could enjoy many visits to Camp Douglas. Unredeemed punches circulated as currency, good for most financial transactions including the weekly collection basket at local churches. (Courtesy of the Chicago Public Library.)

THE POSTMASTER GENERAL AND HIS SON. Cave Johnson (above) of Tennessee served in the U.S. House of Representatives, as a bank president, and as postmaster general of the United States. Nearly 70 years old at the beginning of the Civil War, this eager but elderly Confederate could not join the military; however, his son Polk Johnson served in the Confederate army. As a member of Company A, 49th Tennessee Regiment, Polk fought and was captured at the battle of Fort Donelson. He arrived at Camp Douglas in February 1862 where he stayed until exchanged at Vicksburg in September 1862. While Polk was incarcerated at Camp Douglas, he may have attempted to escape. Such is the observation of a clergyman who saw a package delivered to him containing a Union uniform. (Courtesy of Tennessee State Library and Archives.)

TENT CITY AT CAMP DOUGLAS. Although pressed into service for use as a prison to incarcerate Confederate soldiers almost as soon as paint dried on its newly construction buildings, Camp Douglas's original purpose was to recruit and train Union soldiers. Despite favorable reviews for its modernity, some Union soldiers who lived at Camp Douglas hated the barracks and preferred to sleep in tents. Union parolees brought to Camp Douglas as part of a prisoner exchange set fire to the wooden barracks rather than live in them. Even the Mechanic Fusileers, a regiment of Chicago soldiers who built Camp Douglas, fled the camp. These skilled craftsmen from the Mechanics Institute of Chicago escaped by burning the fences they built surrounding the camp. Members of the 93rd Illinois Infantry refused to stay in the barracks and pitched their tents in a secluded area of Camp Douglas and kept to themselves. (Courtesy of the Chicago History Museum.)

LIFE AT CAMP DOUGLAS BARRACKS. Prisoners lived in long, wooden barracks built to house Union army soldiers during training. Due to a shortage of military guards, prisoners of war could walk freely around the camp, but Chicago's cold, wintry weather forced prisoners who were unaccustomed to ice and snow inside, where they warmed themselves beside stoves. The stoves provided heat and were used to bake johnnycakes with corn meal that was specially purchased for the Southerners. Sick and wounded prisoners were treated at a hospital on the camp's grounds. To supplement their provisions, prisoners of war with extra money could purchase luxuries like tobacco and playing cards from stores operating within Camp Douglas. For entertainment, Confederate army musicians, who were allowed by the Camp Douglas commander to keep their instruments, performed for their fellow prisoners. (Courtesy of the Chicago History Museum.)

PRESIDENTIAL PAROLE. Prisoners with friends in high places, namely the White House, quickly obtained parole from Camp Douglas. As a native-born Kentuckian, Pres. Abraham Lincoln received requests from his fellow Kentuckians to release prisoners. In fact, a group of Kentucky lawyers supplemented their income by charging $100 to contact the president. One request for parole of a spy who served with the Second Kentucky Cavalry arrived just before his execution. The telegraph lines between Washington, D.C., and Chicago crackled with Lincoln's communiques to Camp Douglas commander Colonel Tucker as Lincoln telegraphed him on matters of lesser importance to Confederate prisoners. On August 15, 1862, Tucker received the following telegraph message from the executive mansion: "Is there a prisoner—Dr. Joseph J. Williams? And if so, tell him his wife is here, and allow him to telegraph her. A. Lincoln." (Courtesy of the Library of Congress.)

PLANNERS OF AN ATTACK ON CAMP DOUGLAS. Orders from Jefferson Davis (right), president of the Confederate States of America, led to a plan by Thomas Henry Hines (below) to free prisoners from Camp Douglas during the Democratic National Convention of 1864. The plan included the capture of a federal gunboat patrolling Chicago's Lake Michigan shores, then moored off what is now Cottage Grove Avenue, a choice position for firing upon Camp Douglas's Union guards. With guards dead, the 10,000 Confederate soldiers held as prisoners could easily flee the camp and mount an assault on Chicago. When government officials in Chicago learned about the conspiracy, the Democratic National Convention was postponed for several weeks, foiling the plan. (Right, courtesy of the Filson Historical Society.)

PENNSYLVANIA SOLDIERS. One month after completing training at Camp Cadwalader near Philadelphia, members of the 196th Regiment of the Pennsylvania Infantry arrived at Camp Douglas by railroad. Organized by the Union League Association of Philadelphia and other civic organizations, these so-called "one hundred day men" signed up to serve their country for just 100 days before returning to everyday life as middle-class citizens. Company H, the group pictured here, soon left Chicago for guard duty in Springfield, but other companies of the 196th Pennsylvania Infantry stayed at Camp Douglas long enough to deal with prisoners of war attempting to escape. They recaptured most of the prisoners and put down a rebellion. By the end of their enlistment, 10 members of the Pennsylvania Infantry who served at Camp Douglas died, not from battle wounds, but from diseases including smallpox. (Courtesy of the Chicago History Museum.)

WATER HYDRANT. Despite the abundance of fresh water from nearby Lake Michigan, Camp Douglas prisoners often lacked clean drinking water. According to a prisoner's account published in the Southern Historical Society papers in 1876, "A young man was shot for picking up snow to quench his thirst, when the hydrant had been closed for several days. New and cruel punishments were inflicted, as whim, passion, or pure malignity indicated. . . . Upon one occasion, when a guard discovered a beef bone thrown from the window of number six [barrack], he made all of the prisoners form in line and touch the ground with the fore finger without bending the knee. All who could not do this were beaten. . . . The prisoners were whipped with leather straps and sticks, after the manner of whipping brutes." (Courtesy of the Chicago History Museum.)

MARK SKINNER. While military officials at Camp Douglas eliminated vegetables from prison rations, Chicagoan Mark Skinner, in his capacity as president of the Chicago Sanitary Commission, appealed to Chicagoans to send their homegrown vegetables to Union soldiers fighting in Southern battlefields. In a letter to the *Chicago Tribune*, Skinner wrote, "keep men out of hospitals and save those who are there . . . sickness is increasing, and the free use of vegetables . . . [is] necessary to prevent an epidemic." At a meeting of citizens convened after the battle of Fort Donelson, Skinner voted against sending a large number of medical workers to care for prisoners en route to Camp Douglas. Skinner was not unaware of conditions at Camp Douglas, as he had traveled to Springfield to confer with Gov. Richard Yates about the lack of guards at prison. (Courtesy of *Bygone Days in Chicago*.)

BUTLER THE BEAST. During the Civil War, there was always the expectation that Camp Douglas prisoners would be well cared for until their return to the South. Support for fair treatment of Confederate prisoners held in Camp Douglas came from an unlikely source—a Union general whom some called "Butler the Beast." Gen. Benjamin Franklin Butler earned his nickname for conduct during his occupation of New Orleans. Upset by women who insulted his soldiers, Butler issued General Order No. 28 to treat the ladies of New Orleans as prostitutes. "It is ordered that hereafter when any female shall, by word, gesture, or movement, insult or show contempt for any officer or soldier of the United States, she shall be regarded and held liable to be treated as a woman of the town plying her avocation." Perhaps softened by harsh criticism of the order, Butler advocated for the exchange of sick and wounded prisoners who filled an overcrowded, dirty Camp Douglas.

COL. BENJAMIN J. SWEET. In 1864, Col. Benjamin J. Sweet, a Union army officer from Wisconsin who commanded Camp Douglas, learned of a plan that, in his opinion, threaten the safety of Chicagoans. According to "Intelligence in the Civil War," a report issued by the modern Central Intelligence Agency (CIA), the Confederate States of America spent $5 million to finance a plot by its agents in Canada to free confederate prisoners of war from Camp Douglas. With only 800 men to guard 9,000 prisoners, Sweet may have panicked when he said that Confederate agents "intend to make a night attack on and surprise this camp, release and arm the prisoners of war, cut the telegraph wires, burn the railroad depots, seize the banks and stores containing arms and ammunition, take possession of the city." With the aid of Chicago police, Sweet arrested the conspirators, the Sons of Liberty officers, "along with 106 bushwhackers, guerrillas, and rebel soldiers." (Courtesy of the Chicago History Museum.)

GEORGE ST. LEGER GRENFELL. For his part in the Camp Douglas conspiracy, Col. George St. Leger Grenfell received the death penalty, but as he had many times before, this British citizen cheated death. Under pressure from the British government, Pres. Andrew Johnson commuted Grenfell's sentence to life in a Florida prison. While serving time at Fort Jefferson in the Dry Tortugas, he developed yellow fever, and had it not been for a fellow prisoner who was a physician from Maryland, Grenfell would have died. When Grenfell recovered from yellow fever, he gratefully assisted the doctor with his other patients. Dr. Samuel Mudd, serving time for providing medical aid to John Wilkes Booth, welcomed assistance from Grenfell and the two became lifelong friends until Grenfell drown trying to escape the island prison. (Right, courtesy of the Chicago History Museum.)

COL. G. ST. LEGER GRENFELL,
Hero of the "Black Flag," Chicago Conspirator.

DR. SAMUEL A. MUDD
As He Appeared when Working in the Carpenter's Shop in the Prison at Fort Jefferson

THE LIFE
OF
Dr. Samuel A. Mudd

CONTAINING HIS LETTERS FROM FORT JEFFERSON, DRY TORTUGAS ISLAND, WHERE HE WAS IMPRISONED FOUR YEARS FOR ALLEGED COMPLICITY IN THE ASSASSINATION OF ABRAHAM LINCOLN

WITH

STATEMENTS OF MRS. SAMUEL A. MUDD, DR. SAMUEL A. MUDD, AND EDWARD SPANGLER REGARDING THE ASSASSINATION

AND

THE ARGUMENT OF GENERAL EWING
on the Question of the Jurisdiction of the Military Commission,
and on the Law and Facts of the Case

ALSO "DIARY" OF JOHN WILKES BOOTH

EDITED BY HIS DAUGHTER
NETTIE MUDD

WITH PREFACE BY
D. ELDRIDGE MONROE
OF THE BALTIMORE BAR

New York and Washington
THE NEALE PUBLISHING COMPANY
1906

A BIZARRE METHOD OF PUNISHMENT.
Prisoners who broke Camp Douglas rules were forced to ride the mule, an improvised carpenter's sawhorse made of unfinished boards. As prisoners straddled the mule for hours, the rough wood injured their genitals. Some men who were forced to wear weights tied to their ankles could not walk for days after a ride on the mule. Milton Ryan, a prisoner of war from Mississippi, recalled that the mule stood "about fifteen feet high" and that sometimes prisoners held "a large beef bone in each hand." Infractions punishable by riding the mule included stealing food, cursing, and disobedience. At left is an order sentencing a prisoner of war to ride the mule two hours out of every six for one week. (Above, courtesy of *Bygone Days in Chicago*; left, courtesy of the Chicago History Museum.)

CHICAGO'S HARSH WINTERS. Confederate soldiers who arrived in Chicago during the winter months were not accustomed to the cold weather, and their uniforms were better suited to a Southern climate. Guards used this natural resource to punish disobedient prisoners by forcing men to sit naked in snow banks for hours. Some soldiers suffered from respiratory diseases and frostbite. Surgeons in the camp's hospital amputated damaged limbs, and from November 1864 through February 1865, the death toll at Camp Douglas reached over 1,000, due in part to the hard winter. Through churches and charitable organizations, compassionate women of Chicago donated blankets and warm underwear to the prisoners of war. A suggestion to provide prisoners with heavy uniforms rejected by the Union army due to poor quality was considered and dismissed when it was realized that prisoners of war wearing Union uniforms easily would find their way out of Camp Douglas. (Courtesy of *Bygone Days in Chicago*.)

ESCAPEES PUNISHED. Hundreds of prisoners attempted to escape by digging tunnels, climbing the fence, or walking out the door wearing newly-acquired civilian clothing. Some were successful. Those who were not were punished or shot to death. Some prisoners who attempted to escape from Camp Douglas were punished by wearing a ball and chain. Milton Ryan, a prisoner of war from Mississippi, described the punishment. "The chain was riveted around the ankle and the ball at the other end of the chain. It was almost as much as the poor fellow could carry. That was one thing that stuck closer than a brother. It went with him by day and by night, and even lay by his side in his cold naked bunk at night." The cannon balls attached to the prisoners weighed over 30 pounds. (Courtesy of *Bygone Days in Chicago*.)

THE DUNGEON AT CAMP DOUGLAS. Conditions in the White Oak Dungeon, a prison within a prison, were so putrid that a physician nearly passed out while inspecting the facility. Milton Ryan of Mississippi, who spent time in the dungeon for fetching water from the wrong well recalls, "It was a guard house made of white oak logs twelve or fourteen inches in diameter . . . a pair of steps led down into this dark foul hole. It was pitch dark in there; one could not see his hand before him when the door was closed." In 1863, twenty-six desperate prisoners escaped from the White Oak Dungeon by way of a tunnel they dug beneath a garbage dump. At right is an order directing guards to feed, until further notice, only bread and water to a prisoner held in the White Oak Dungeon for insubordination. (Courtesy of the Chicago History Museum.)

MORGAN'S RAIDERS. Kentucky cavalrymen known as Morgan's Raiders, named for Gen. John Hunt Morgan, worked diligently to escape and return to battle. One of Morgan's Raiders, Samuel G. Grasty of Virginia, simply walked out of Camp Douglas to a friend's house downtown and boarded a train for Richmond, but his fellow soldiers had to work harder to escape. One group of Morgan's Raiders dug their way out of the dungeon, which was an extra-security prison, drawing admiration from guards for their ingenuity. Others hid their tools in a haystack at night and by daylight dug tunnels from beneath their bunks to the other side of the perimeter fence. To discourage further escape attempts, the camp commander removed wooden floors from the barracks and hung a group of soldiers by their thumbs. Morgan escaped from the Ohio State Penitentiary with several of his officers—the only successful escape from that prison during the 19th century. (Courtesy of the Chicago History Museum.)

HENRY WAGER HALLECK. Despite his shy, awkward appearance, West Point–trained Gen. Henry W. Halleck (right) served 15 years active duty in the Union army and, at the time of the battle of Fort Donelson, was the superior of Ulysses S. Grant (below). Pres. Abraham Lincoln appointed Halleck as Union commander in chief and chief of staff of the armies of the United States. As such, Halleck disapproved of the selection of former newspaper owner Col. Daniel Cameron as commander of Camp Douglas and requested Cameron's immediate termination. After Cameron's departure, Halleck took drastic measures at Camp Douglas. In April 1862, Halleck ordered the confinement of escapees to Camp Douglas's dungeon. As a cost-saving measure, he reduced food rations for all prisoners and allowed only the sick and wounded meager amounts of tea, coffee, and sugar.

OVERCROWDING AT CAMP DOUGLAS. The exact number of prisoners who lived and died at Camp Douglas remains unknown due to faulty recordkeeping; however, scholars who specialize in the history of Camp Douglas pieced together the following statistics from contemporaneous reports and government files: maximum capacity was 4,500 prisoners; the largest number of prisoners held at one time was 12,080; the total number of Confederate prisoners incarcerated at

Camp Douglas was 26,000; the number of cases of serious disease such as pneumonia, smallpox, and malaria reached 70,088; the number of hospital beds at Camp Douglas was 300; and the number of Confederate soldiers who died at Camp Douglas was 6,000. (Courtesy of the Chicago History Museum.)

BEEF SCANDAL. Independent contractors eager to earn money in wartime vied to obtain agreements to provide Camp Douglas with food and other supplies. Prisoners who complained about the poor quality of meat (gristle and bone) served at Camp Douglas were not taken seriously until officials discovered the exorbitant prices they paid for inferior beef. The matter reached Pres. Abraham Lincoln, who knew one of the suppliers, his brother-in-law Ninian W. Edwards of Springfield. In fact, it was through Edward's wife, Elizabeth, Mary Todd Lincoln's sister, that young Lincoln met his future wife, Mary Todd. Embarrassed by the beef scandal, the brothers-in-law fired off a series of angry letters to each other until the problem was resolved. (Below, Courtesy of the Abraham Lincoln Presidential Library.)

OLD SOLDIERS' HOME. To provide long-term care for disabled Civil War soldiers, the Chicago Sanitary Commission raised money to build the Old Soldiers' Home on Thirty-fifth Street next to Camp Douglas. Guests at the official opening on July 4, 1863, included the Camp Douglas post surgeon and post chaplain. Within a few days, healthy Union soldiers who guarded Camp Douglas descended upon the Old Soldier's Home kitchen demanding food to supplement their meager rations. The practice was quickly stopped but, in 1864, eighty soldiers from Camp Douglas attending a funeral on the hospital grounds stayed for lunch, which, according to a report in the *Chicago Tribune*, "they claimed was much better than they got at Camp." (Above, courtesy of the Chicago Public Library; below, author's collection.)

Isaac N. Hunt. The extraordinary sight of 1,000 cavalrymen as they roared into tiny Scottsville, Kentucky, was enough to convince young Isaac N. Hunt to join Morgan's Raiders. After an impassioned speech by Gen. John Hunt Morgan at the Scottsville Hotel, Hunt joined up. Convinced of the sincerity of Morgan's message that the men of Kentucky should join the Confederate cause, Hunt left his family's home and rode off. As a private in Company C, 3rd Kentucky Cavalry, the teenager fought for more than one year until he was captured and sent to Camp Douglas. Despite the tortuous treatment doled out to Morgan's Raiders at Camp Douglas, Hunt lived for 50 years after the Civil War ended and died when he was nearly 70 years old. (Courtesy of Campbellsville University.)

BUCKNER STITH MORRIS. Buckner Stith Morris, one of two Chicago mayors imprisoned at Camp Douglas, served as mayor of the city from 1838 to 1839. A Southerner by birth, Morris sympathized with copperheads, northern Democrats who opposed the war. Arrested on suspicion of plotting to free Camp Douglas prisoners of war, he was imprisoned in Camp Douglas and tried by a military court that acquitted him of all charges. While awaiting trial in Ohio, Morris's daughter died. Also arrested in the conspiracy trial was his wife, Mary, who had supplied pickles and potatoes to prisoners afflicted with scurvy. She was found guilty and banished to live in Kentucky; however, she was allowed to return to Chicago for her husband's funeral. Morris is buried at Rosehill Cemetery on Chicago's North Side. (Courtesy of the Chicago Public Library.)

THE LATE ALLAN PINKERTON.

ALLAN PINKERTON. Scottish immigrant Allan Pinkerton was among those private citizens who uncovered the conspiracy that led to the arrest of Buckner Stith Morris and his wife, Mary Morris.

DETECTIVE THWARTS ESCAPE PLAN.
Allan Pinkerton moved to Chicago where he formed the first American detective agency and was the first to be called a private eye. People referred to him as a private eye because of the logo on his downtown headquarters that had a large graphic of an eye and the slogan We Never Sleep. The Pinkerton Detective Agency became famous when it foiled an assassination plot against president-elect Abraham Lincoln. In 1864, when word of a conspiracy to revolt at Camp Douglas reached the agency, Pinkerton's guards infiltrated the camp and fed information to the Union army.

OBSERVATORY AS LOOKOUT TOWER. Tipped off to a conspiracy to attack Camp Douglas, Col. Benjamin J. Sweet stationed riflemen on the Dearborn Observatory tower on the University of Chicago campus located at 3400 South Cottage Grove Avenue in Chicago, adjacent to Camp Douglas. Sweet's riflemen were familiar with the grounds as they used it for hunting wild game until forbidden by University of Chicago officials. The 90-foot tower housed what was, at the time, the largest telescope in the world. The telescope was moved to the Evanston campus of Northwestern University in 1887 and is in use today. It is available to the public for stargazing on Friday evenings. (Courtesy of the Chicago Public Library.)

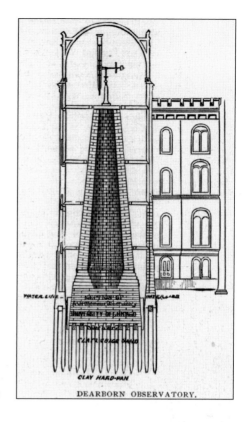

DEARBORN OBSERVATORY.

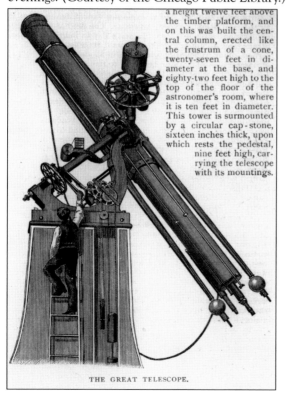

a height twelve feet above the timber platform, and on this was built the central column, erected like the frustrum of a cone, twenty-seven feet in diameter at the base, and eighty-two feet high to the top of the floor of the astronomer's room, where it is ten feet in diameter. This tower is surmounted by a circular cap-stone, sixteen inches thick, upon which rests the pedestal, nine feet high, carrying the telescope with its mountings.

THE GREAT TELESCOPE.

GEN. AMBROSE E. BURNSIDE. The man whose primary legacy is having sideburns named for him, so strongly opposed Southern sympathizers that he considered it treason, an offence punishable by death. Gen. Ambrose E. Burnside issued Order No. 38, which stated, "The habit of declaring sympathy for the enemy will not be allowed in this department. Persons committing such offenses will be at once arrested with a view of being tried . . . or sent beyond our lines into the lines of their friends. It must be understood that treason, expressed or implied, will not be tolerated in this department." Despite Burnside's fierce beliefs, he found the conditions at Camp Douglas deplorable and called for its closure.

STOP THE PRESSES. The sale of the *Chicago Times* was banned at Camp Douglas for its Southern views, but the competing newspaper, the *Chicago Tribune*, could be purchased by prisoners. Wilbur Fiske Storey, owner and editor of the *Chicago Times* stated, "It is a newspaper's job to print the news and raise hell." In retaliation for expressing his views in print during the Civil War, Burnside ordered the commander of Camp Douglas to close down the *Chicago Times*. Reporters were arrested by the military and the newspaper ceased publishing briefly. Storey delighted in the notoriety gained by the seizure of his newspaper and continued to publish his views, calling the Emancipation Proclamation monstrous, "It will be known in all history as the most wicked, atrocious and revolting deed recorded in the annals of civilization." Storey's men reported on conditions at Camp Douglas, including accounts of prisoners freezing to death. Storey also called for the closure of Camp Douglas. (Courtesy of *Bygone Days in Chicago*.)

Isaac Newton Arnold. In June 1863, Congressman Isaac Newton Arnold of Chicago was asked to contact his friend Pres. Abraham Lincoln to lift Gen. Ambrose E. Burnside's order to close the *Chicago Times*. The president revoked the order; however, his action was not taken at the behest of Arnold, who claimed he had not read the *Chicago Times* in several weeks. Once on opposite sides of the "Great Sand Bar case," a lawsuit to determine ownership of lakefront property, the pair became friends. At the 1863 Northwest Sanitary Fair in Chicago, Arnold awarded the president a $200 gold watch, the prize for the largest contributor. The president's draft of the Emancipation Proclamation fetched $3,000. The president was unable to attend, so ladies of the fair brought the watch to the White House. Arnold died in 1884 and was buried in Graceland Cemetery. (Courtesy of the Library of Congress.)

DRAINAGE OF SWAMPY CAMP VETOED.
Montgomery Cunningham Meigs, for
whom Chicago's defunct lakeshore airport
was named, served as the U.S. Army
quartermaster for more than 20 years.
As an army captain in the 1850s, Meigs
supervised the construction of an aqueduct
system for Washington, D.C., by the
Army Corps of Engineers. His Civil War
responsibilities included moving nearly
one million troops and millions of tons of
supplies. Meigs vowed to provide supplies to
prisoners with "the strictest economy" and
expected the prisoners of war to furnish
their own clothing. This was impractical
for prisoners who arrived at Camp Douglas
wearing clothes unsuitable for winter. As
its population grew, urine from men and
horses flowed through the camp. Citing
the high cost of sewers, Meigs rejected a
proposal to improve sanitation at Camp
Douglas and suggested instead that
prisoners clean up after themselves. Despite
his treatment of prisoners, he was a devoted
father to his children (above). (Courtesy of
the Library of Congress.)

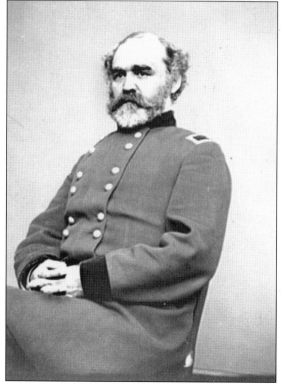

HOYNE'S RESOLUTION TO CLOSE CAMP DOUGLAS. Thousands of Camp Douglas prisoners of war contracted smallpox and hundreds were buried in a cemetery on the grounds. Infected patients regularly escaped from the camp's smallpox hospital, tempted by lax security. Worried parents began withdrawing their children and their funds from the University of Chicago next door. Because of the sharp drop in enrollment, the board met to demand closure of Camp Douglas. Thomas Hoyne, who financed the university's $18,000 telescope and whose son Temple attended the university, was asked to present to government officials the school's demand for the closure of Camp Douglas. The camp did not close; however, the University of Chicago relocated to Hyde Park. While Hoyne was unsuccessful in this endeavor, he convinced voters to elect him mayor of Chicago. (Courtesy of *Bygone Days in Chicago.*)

MAYOR SENT TO PRISON. By the time Daniel Boone's grandnephew Dr. Levi Day Boone landed in the Camp Douglas prison for aiding prisoners, he was elected as a Chicago mayor and the first president of the Chicago Medical Society. As mayor, he established the city's first police force to protect the public. He then infuriated his constituents by banning alcohol on Sundays and increasing the cost of liquor licenses issued to taverns. As crowds of angry voters swarmed towards city hall in the Lager Beer Riot of 1855, Boone ordered swing bridges opened to prevent the crowds from crossing the Chicago River, injuring many who were caught on them. A Kentuckian by birth, Boone sympathized with the South and collected clothing for prisoners at Camp Douglas. (Courtesy of the Chicago Public Library.)

EDWIN M. STANTON. In September 1862, the secretary of war (left) received a letter from the president of the United States regarding the imprisonment at Camp Douglas of former Chicago mayor Dr. Levi Day Boone that stated, "I personally know Dr. Levi D. Boone, of Chicago, Illinois, who is not in close confinement, but on limits, on parol [sic], under bonds, and oath of allegiance. From my knowledge of him, and the open, and rather marked part he has taken for the war, I think he should be at least, enlarged generally, on the same terms. If the Sec. of War concurs, let it be done. Yours truly A. Lincoln." Boone (below) spent more than one month imprisoned at Camp Douglas for allegedly supplying indigent confederate prisoners with money to purchase food and other necessities from Camp Douglas vendors. (Left, courtesy of *Bygone Days in Chicago*.)

ELLIS SYLVESTER CHESBROUGH. The City of Chicago hired engineer Ellis Sylvester Chesbrough to solve its water supply problems. During the Civil War, he began work on a water crib and a two-mile tunnel beneath Lake Michigan to bring fresh lake water to residents and, later, he reversed the flow of the Chicago River. At the request of the Chicago Board of Public Works, Chesbrough was sent to Camp Douglas to inspect its sanitary systems of drains and toilets. The swampy soil caused by Camp Douglas's proximity to Lake Michigan was one of many sources of unsanitary conditions at the camp, yet while local newspapers reported daily on the death of prisoners from unsanitary conditions, Chesbrough congratulated the Camp Douglas commander on his attention to sanitation, saying the camp was cleaner than the rest of Chicago. (Right, courtesy of the Chicago Public Library; below, courtesy of the Chicago History Museum.)

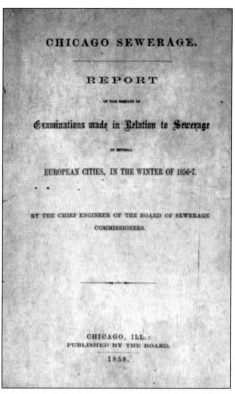

CHICAGO SEWERAGE.

REPORT

OF THE RESULTS OF

Examinations made in Relation to Sewerage

IN SEVERAL

EUROPEAN CITIES, IN THE WINTER OF 1856-7.

BY THE CHIEF ENGINEER OF THE BOARD OF SEWERAGE COMMISSIONERS.

CHICAGO, ILL.:
PUBLISHED BY THE BOARD.
1858.

VIEW OF AN ENTIRE BLOCK OF BRICK & STONE BUILDINGS IN CHICAGO ON LAKE ST. BETWEEN CLARK & LASALLE STRS. WHILE BEING RAISED TO THE NEW GRADE A HIGHT OF 4 FEET.

FIRES DELIBERATE AND ACCIDENTAL. Upon inspecting living conditions at Camp Douglas, the president of the United States Sanitary Commission declared, "The barracks were so filthy and infested, that nothing but fire can cleanse them." Ironically the city's horse-drawn fire engines appeared at Camp Douglas throughout its history. Cooking stoves were temporarily banned after small fires damaged wooden kitchens. On one occasion, the fence surrounding the camp burned, allowing prisoners to escape; however, all escapees were returned by Native American guards who were given "shoot to kill" orders. Union soldiers sent to Camp Douglas as part of a prisoner exchange agreed with the United States Sanitary Commission. They set fire to the barracks. Chicago firefighters did their best to extinguish the fire, but the barracks burned to the ground, so Union soldiers pitched tents on the swampy land. In the summer of 1864, officials installed a fire hydrant inside the camp to make firefighting more efficient. (Courtesy of the Chicago Public Library.)

MILITARY TRIAL OF CIVILIANS. One of the most comprehensive accounts of the Camp Douglas conspiracy trial comes from Dr. I. Winslow Ayer, a Chicago physician whose newspaper advertisements claimed that, with his medicines, "improvement is felt at once." While working in his office downtown, Ayer overheard a conversation in the next room that led him to infiltrate a group planning to free Camp Douglas prisons. When he testified at the trial in Cincinnati, he kept Chicagoans informed and later supplemented his income by selling his book, *The Great Treason Plot In the North During the War.* He modestly referred to himself as, "the Preserver of the City of Chicago," a "Daring Officer of Secret Service," and "the only man living who can give all the thrilling facts." (Courtesy of the Chicago History Museum.)

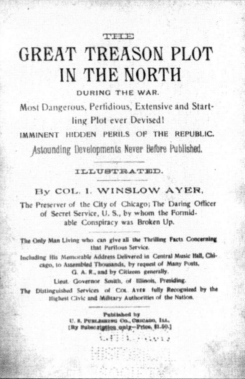

THE

GREAT TREASON PLOT
IN THE NORTH

DURING THE WAR.

Most Dangerous, Perfidious, Extensive and Startling Plot ever Devised!

IMMINENT HIDDEN PERILS OF THE REPUBLIC.

Astounding Developments Never Before Published.

ILLUSTRATED.

By COL. I. WINSLOW AYER,

The Preserver of the City of Chicago; The Daring Officer of Secret Service, U. S., by whom the Formidable Conspiracy was Broken Up.

The Only Man Living who can give all the Thrilling Facts Concerning that Perilous Service.

Including His Memorable Address Delivered in Central Music Hall, Chicago, to Assembled Thousands, by request of Many Posts, G. A. R., and by Citizens generally.

Lieut. Governor Smith, of Illinois, Presiding.

The Distinguished Services of Col. Ayer fully Recognized by the Highest Civic and Military Authorities of the Nation.

Published by
U. S. PUBLISHING CO., CHICAGO, ILL.
[By Subscription only.—Price, $1.50.]

APRIL 1865. The surrender of Confederate general Robert E. Lee did not go unnoticed in Chicago. When word of the surrender at Appomattox reached Chicago, the Dearborn Light Artillery fired 100 guns into the air, frightening sleepy residents. Businesses closed for a day of celebration and Col. Benjamin J. Sweet gave a speech at Camp Douglas; however, celebrations were quickly cut short upon receiving news of the assassination of Pres. Abraham Lincoln. To honor the president, Sweet ordered the flag at Camp Douglas to be lowered, but something went terribly wrong when a Union soldier became tangled in the pulley and fell to his death. Prisoners applauded. (Courtesy of the Library of Congress.)

PRES. ABRAHAM LINCOLN'S REMAINS IN CHICAGO. As the funeral train carrying the body of Lincoln reached Chicago's South Side, wounded soldiers from the Old Soldiers' Home and Union guards from Camp Douglas gathered to give the president a silent salute. When the funeral train reached downtown, Sweet and Gen. Joseph Hooker joined the solemn procession along the crowded streets. Chicagoans viewed the remains in the new courthouse at the rate of 17,000 per hour, and many noticed a discoloration of the president's face. When the funeral train departed for its final stop in Springfield, Hooker accompanied the body. (Courtesy of the Chicago Public Library.)

CHARLES WALSH. When the Civil War began, Chicago businessman Charles Walsh supported the Union, with his bank account and his actions. However, by the end of the war, Walsh, a civilian, was imprisoned by a military court for supporting the Confederates. This Irish immigrant joined with Col. James A. Mulligan to form the Irish Brigade, but angered by Pres. Abraham Lincoln's Emancipation Proclamation, Walsh was determined to overthrow the Union government with the help of Camp Douglas prisoners that he planned to free. Caught up in a conspiracy hatched by Confederate agents living in Canada, Walsh was arrested in his Chicago home where Camp Douglas officers and Chicago police found a large cache of weapons and ammunition. One of Walsh's daughters, Letitia, testified at her father's trial that the guns "were to protect Democrats at the polls," and that her father could not afford to keep her in boarding school because he spent the family's money to support Union regiments. A judge who thought otherwise handed Walsh a five-year prison sentence, but Walsh was pardoned. (Courtesy of the Chicago History Museum.)

Four

THE NORTH'S LARGEST CONFEDERATE CEMETERY

North America's largest mass grave is filled with the remains of over 6,000 Confederate soldiers who were held as prisoners at Camp Douglas. The location of this mass grave is not in a tourist site like Gettysburg National Military Park or a famous military cemetery such as Arlington National Cemetery. It is located a short distance from a Chicago Transit Authority bus stop in Oak Woods Cemetery on Chicago's South Side.

After the Civil War ended, Chicago faced the problem of disposing of more than 6,000 bodies of Confederate soldiers who died at Camp Douglas. The closure of Camp Douglas in November 1865 necessitated the removal of bodies buried in its small cemetery. The City Cemetery on the shores of Lake Michigan was in the process of becoming Lincoln Park, and bodies had to be moved. Chicago civilians buried there over a 30-year period were dug up and reburied in cemeteries around Chicago. Because no cemetery in Chicago wanted Confederate soldiers buried in its soil, Oak Woods Cemetery, which was outside the city limits at the time, was selected.

And still, the dead did not rest peacefully. Their bodies sank in the swampy soil and some floated into Lake Michigan. The weight of the heavy monument dedicated in 1895 damaged the grave site. And the names of the dead did not appear on the grave site until mandated by federal legislation in 1912.

FUNERAL PARLOR ON CAMP DOUGLAS GROUNDS. African American Charles H. Griffin enlisted as a private in Company B, 29th Regiment of the U.S. Colored Infantry in January 1864, a few months after the first Illinois regiment of African Americans was authorized. When his grandson Ernest Griffin moved the family funeral parlor business to a new location, the family realized it was the former site of Camp Douglas where their grandfather Charles H. had trained. As a tribute to Camp Douglas soldiers, Union and Confederate, Ernest began the practice of raising Union and Confederate flags and built a small museum on the funeral parlor's property. During its history, the Griffin Funeral Home, which continues to operate under the direction of the Griffin family, has waked many famous African Americans, including murder victim Emmett Till and Pulitzer prize–winning poet Gwendolyn Brooks. (Author's collection.)

GROVELAND PARK. In an effort to erase all traces of Camp Douglas, land was sold to developers to build post–Civil War homes. One of these communities, Groveland Park, lies tucked behind a shopping mall and high-rise apartment buildings, where access to Groveland Park Avenue is closely guarded by a groundskeeper who lives in a tiny cottage at the entrance of the road. Wealthy Chicagoans such as Joy Morton, who founded the Morton Salt Company, snapped up the newly-built stately mansions in Groveland Park. Groveland Park Avenue, a small, winding road, runs through a grove of tall trees designated as a park in perpetuity by the estate of Stephen A. Douglas. (Author's collection.)

CAMP DOUGLAS BUILDINGS. At the end of the Civil War, Camp Douglas extant buildings included four hospitals, officers' quarters, three warehouses, a church, 64 prisoners' barracks, 40 garrison barracks, a combination laundry and bathhouse, and a Civil War–era shopping mall consisting of a pharmacy, general store, tool shop, and post office. Some wooden buildings, such as this one, remained intact for a few years, but most were demolished due to public pressure to remove traces of a Confederate presence in Chicago. Also real estate developers, including former mayor "Long John" Wentworth, were eager to build homes on land conveniently located near a railroad station, a short commute for prospective buyers who owned businesses downtown. However, some civil-minded individuals argued for keeping the hospitals open to indigent Chicagoans. The *Chicago Tribune* reported the hospitals were "especially large and commodious, containing accommodations for over three hundred," and provided "all comforts for the sick." (Courtesy of the Chicago History Museum.)

DOUGLAS FAMILY PROPERTY. Despite substantial financial wealth and real estate holdings prior to the death of Sen. Stephen A. Douglas, executors of his estate were forced to negotiate with creditors and sell his property to pay the family's bills. The Circuit Court of Cook County, Chancery Division held a hearing on the foreclosure of the $11,000 mortgage on Douglas's home on Cottage Grove Avenue, and subsequent owners of the house faced further issues in local courts regarding the property. While the senator's sons unsuccessfully fought to recover damages from the federal government for raiding their Mississippi cotton plantation, their stepmother, Adele, received $25,000 from the Illinois government for the purchase of land to build a monument dedicated to her husband. Within a few years after the death of Douglas, his widow, Adele, left Chicago with her new husband, Robert Williams. (Courtesy of the Chicago History Museum.)

MAY 30, 1895. Unusual circumstances brought Pres. Grover Cleveland to Chicago and placed him between hundreds of Union and Confederate soldiers, an experience he had avoided during the Civil War by paying a surrogate to take his place. It happened on May 30, 1895, in Chicago's Oak Woods Cemetery. Cleveland arrived in Chicago to attend funeral services for U.S. Secretary of State Walter Quinton Gresham, a distinguished Civil War veteran. Strongly criticized for not visiting his secretary of state as he succumbed to death, Cleveland and his cabinet resolutely boarded a train to attend the funeral. By coincidence, hundreds of Confederate veterans arrived at the cemetery for the dedication of a monument to honor Confederate soldiers who died at Camp Douglas. (Below, author's collection.)

THE UNDERTAKER AND THE LAKE.
C. H. Jordan, a prominent Chicago
undertaker, received $4.75 per body
to bury Camp Douglas's prisoners of
war. Although thousands of bodies
were buried at the City Cemetery
(now Lincoln Park) and hundreds in
the Camp Douglas smallpox cemetery,
historians suspect that Jordan's
subcontractors sold dozens of bodies to
prestigious medical schools or threw
them into Lake Michigan. In January
1863, the body of a baby was found
floating in the lake near Camp Douglas,
and it was sent to Jordan's undertaking
parlor on Clark Street. For years after
the Civil War ended, bodies continued
to wash up on shore and bob along the
city's new water crib. (Right, courtesy
of the Chicago History Museum; below,
courtesy of the Chicago Public Library.)

OAK WOODS CEMETERY. Commuters who ride the No. 67 Chicago Transit Authority bus to Cottage Grove Avenue may be aware of some of the famous residents of this Chicago cemetery, such as Chicago's first African American mayor, Harold Washington; Olympic gold medal winner Jesse Owens; and Giacomo "Big Jim" Colosimo, the gangster who ran Chicago's crime syndicate until he was dethroned by Al Capone. These men were buried with pomp and circumstance among other Chicagoans, including Mayor William Hale Thompson; Mayor Monroe Heath; Illinois governor John Marshall Hamilton; Illinois governor Charles Samuel Deneen; physicist Enrico Fermi, who was known as the father of the atomic bomb; Bishop Louis Henry Ford, for whom the Bishop Ford Freeway was named; and others. Yet most Chicago commuters are unaware of the 6,000 Confederate prisoners of war buried together in North America's largest mass grave. (Photographs by Joseph Pucci.)

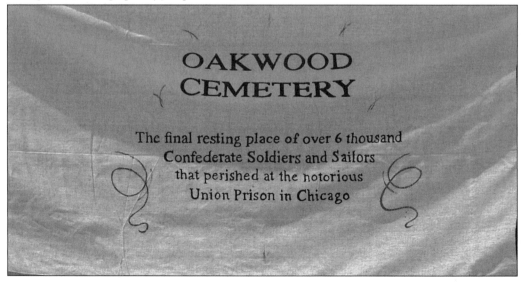

ROSEHILL CEMETERY. The closure of City Cemetery, where thousands of Camp Douglas prisoners of war were buried, necessitated the quick removal of bodies, but finding a Chicago cemetery that permitted the burial of Confederate soldiers was a problem. Rosehill Cemetery, with its cathedral-like entrance that was designed by William Boyington, who also designed Chicago's famous Water Tower, was among the area cemeteries considered for the final resting place of Camp Douglas prisoners of war. During its heyday, the railroad line operated a midday funeral train for mourners. This busy cemetery, located approximately seven miles from the Loop, is still easily reached by railroad. Gen. Montgomery C. Meigs rejected Rosehill Cemetery, citing the price of $600 per acre of land as too expensive. Despite Meigs's rejection of Rosehill Cemetery, Camp Douglas prisoners of war who died after the Civil War ended were buried there, but not at his expense. Col. Benjamin J. Sweet, one of the commanders of Camp Douglas, and two of its most famous prisoners, Mayor Levi Day Boone and Mayor Buckner Morris, are also buried here. (Author's collection.)

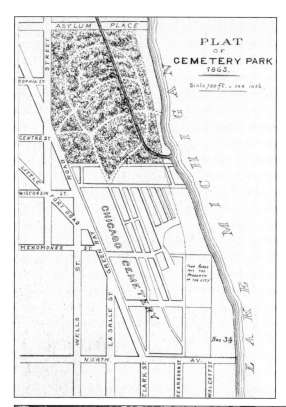

CITY CEMETERY AND COUCH MAUSOLEUM. Bodies buried in City Cemetery, including thousands of Camp Douglas prisoners of war, were removed to make way for Lincoln Park after the assassination of Pres. Abraham Lincoln. With the Civil War at an end but anti-Confederate sentiments in Chicago still high, military officials scrambled to remove bodies hastily buried in the sandy soil. Fewer bodies than expected were recovered; some had washed into the waters of Lake Michigan and were never found. Curiously one tomb remains near the Chicago History Museum; the grave site of Ira Couch, owner of the Tremont House Hotel. The hotel was a favorite of Abraham Lincoln, the location where Stephen A. Douglas died, and where Col. Elmer Ephraim Ellsworth's Zouaves paraded. (Left, courtesy of the Chicago Public Library; below, author's collection.)

110

CONFEDERATE DAUGHTER. Sharon L. Welzen appears in period dress at a 2007 Sons of Confederate Veterans ceremony honoring Camp Douglas prisoners of war buried at Oak Woods Cemetery in Chicago. During the annual ceremony, ladies of the Sons of Confederate Veterans, Illinois Division, Camp Douglas Memorial No. 1507, place roses on the Confederate Mound to honor their ancestors, and afterwards they uphold a Civil War traditional of offering a picnic lunch of fried chicken and other Southern dishes to friends and family. Welzen, who traced her family roots to great uncles who served in the Confederate army, designed her dress of lightweight wool. (Author's collection.)

MILITARY SALUTE AT OAK WOODS CEMETERY. The Sons of Confederate Veterans, Illinois Division, Camp Douglas Memorial No. 1507, salute the Confederate prisoners of war buried at Oak Woods Cemetery in Chicago. The group, which consisted of descendents of Confederate soldiers who served from 1861 through 1865, performed in period uniform at an annual program at Oak Woods Cemetery. In addition to a military salute, the group scattered soil taken from the states represented by the monument. The group also conducts ceremonies at other military cemeteries in Illinois, including Rosehill Cemetery on the city's North Side where Camp Douglas prisoners of war who died after the Civil War were buried. (Author's collection.)

DISPLAY OF WEAPONS AT OAK WOODS CEMETERY. In 1895, federal legislation introduced by Congressman James Robert Mann authorized the appropriation of $3,850 to repair the Confederate burial site and to bring to Oak Woods Cemetery cannons and cannonballs that remain on display today. A crowd of over 100,000 witnessed the May 30, 1895, unveiling of the artifacts that, despite rumors, were not taken from Camp Douglas. The cannonballs are the type tied to the ankles of Camp Douglas prisoners who disobeyed rules, however, the cannons were fired during the Civil War by both the North and the South. (Author's collection.)

CAMP DOUGLAS GUARDS BURIED WITH PRISONERS. Wagonloads of bodies were hastily removed from Camp Douglas a few years after the Civil War and little was done to keep accurate and comprehensive records identifying the remains of the deceased. In a gruesome twist of fate, the remains of 12 Union soldiers were piled in a heap with the remains of Camp Douglas prisoners and brought by a horse-drawn wagon from a small cemetery on the Camp Douglas grounds to the Oak Woods Cemetery. Hospital records indicate that nearly two dozen Union soldiers died at Camp Douglas, but without uniforms and burned to prevent diseases from spreading, the identities of the 12 men buried at Oak Woods are unknown. Some historians believe these Union soldiers guarded, and perhaps punished, the Confederate soldiers buried together on the Confederate Mound. (Author's collection.)

NAMES OF THE DEAD. Although over 6,000 Confederate prisoners of war who died at Camp Douglas are buried at Chicago's Oak Woods Cemetery on the city's South Side, no names identify the soldiers buried in the mass grave, and only 4,243 names appear on the grave today. It was not until 1912 that names of the deceased were added, when a federal law requiring all graves of Confederate soldiers to be identified with grave markers was passed. To accommodate 16 bronze plaques on which the names appear, the Confederate Mound was raised several feet, and a granite plinth was added in 1912. The task of identifying and marking graves of Confederate soldiers is an ongoing process continued by the Sons of Confederate Veterans. (Author's collection.)

HEADSTONE OF JAMES W. LEAK. Among the 4,243 names etched on the Confederate Mound monument at Chicago's Oak Woods Cemetery is the following: Joseph W. Leak, Company C, First Regiment, Alabama Infantry, Confederate States of America, died February 10, 1865. This entry is incorrect; the soldier's name is James W. Leak. To rectify the mistake, a headstone bearing the correct name was placed at the edge of the grave site. Two other of Camp Douglas's prisoners of war received special treatment after death. Although Oak Woods Cemetery's Jewish section opened in 1854, Pvt. Theodore Hirsch, a Jewish prisoner of war from Louisiana who died at Camp Douglas in 1864, was buried in Chicago's Hebrew Benevolent Society Cemetery, part of Graceland. Finally Pvt. James Lyons, a Catholic from Tennessee, is buried in Calvary Cemetery, a Catholic cemetery in suburban Evanston. (Author's collection.)

THE UNION GRAVEYARD AT OAK WOODS CEMETERY. Located in a section of Chicago's Oak Woods Cemetery far from the Confederate Mound, there is a statue of Pres. Abraham Lincoln surrounded by a small group of graves, each bearing the name of a Union soldier. The statue is the work of Charles Mulligan, an Irish immigrant who studied with Lorado Taft. Taft founded Chicago's Palette and Chisel Club and taught sculpture at the Art Institute of Chicago. The statue, which depicts the president speaking at Gettysburg, is actually a smaller version of the original Mulligan sculpted for Pana. The statue was purchased and installed in Oak Wood Cemetery by the Grand Army of the Republic in 1905. (Author's collection.)

THE CONFEDERATE MOUND AT OAK WOODS CEMETERY. The Confederate grave site at Oak Woods Cemetery on Chicago's South Side that visitors see today bears little resemblance to the original where over 6,000 bodies of Confederate prisoners who died at Camp Douglas were buried in a mass grave. The grounds are well kept, in part by the staff of the Oak Woods Cemetery, the Sons of Confederate Veterans who hold a memorial service annually at the end of April, and the federal government that, by law, provides an annual maintenance budget of $250. The original grave site, named the Confederate Mound because it actually was a mound, sank in wet soil and had to be rebuilt. (Author's collection.)

MARSHY, SWAMPY LAND. The Stephen A. Douglas monument was built on land adjacent to Camp Douglas that had been owned by Douglas. Photographs taken at the monument in 2007 show marshy land caused by its close proximity to Lake Michigan. These wet conditions caused great hardships for the Confederate prisoners held at Camp Douglas. Rabbits, birds, and butterflies live among the old trees and newly planted flower beds maintained by the State of Illinois. (Author's collection.)

A Current View of Camp Douglas. The Lake Meadows Shopping Center, located at Thirty-fifth Street and Martin Luther King Jr. Drive, is shown here in a 2007 photograph. It bears little resemblance to the prison that held thousands of Confederate soldiers during the Civil War. The area around the shopping center is densely populated with high-rise apartment buildings and, according to the 2000 U.S. census, the population within a one-miles radius was more than 45,000 people. (Author's collection.)

LEONARD VOLK'S SCULPTURES. Four bronze statues of women surround the base of the Stephen A. Douglas monument designed by Leonard Volk. The women represent eloquence, justice, Illinois, and history. Justice is pictured in this 2007 photograph. Bas reliefs depicting different aspects of the senator's life appear behind the statues. (Author's collection.)

THE OLD SOLDIERS' HOME TODAY.
In its history, the building next to
Camp Douglas served as a hospital for
severely wounded Union soldiers until
1872 when it was turned over to the
Sisters of St. Joseph of Carondelet who
reopened the building as an orphanage.
In the latter part of the 20th century,
troubled youths received psychological
counseling at the facility, and in 1996,
the City of Chicago gave the building
landmark status. The building, which
is located directly across the street from
the Stephen A. Douglas monument, is
currently closed. (Author's collection.)

OAKENWALD. The Stephen A. Douglas monument was built on property formerly owned by the senator. Calling his estate Oakenwald, he intended to build a grand home for his family, stables, and all other buildings needed for a gentlemen's life. Douglas died before he was able to complete his plans. (Author's collection.)

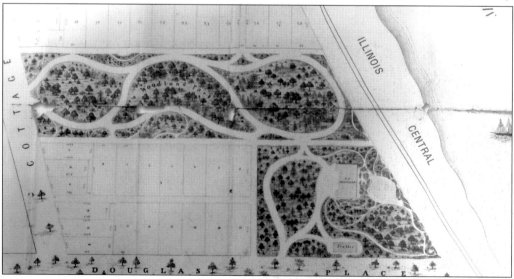

THE TOMB OF STEPHEN A. DOUGLAS.
In life, Sen. Stephen A. Douglas was a little man; in death, he is nearly nine feet tall. The statue of Douglas, which stands atop a 96-foot-tall granite structure, faces east overlooking the tracks of the Illinois Central Railroad and Lake Michigan. The interior of the tomb is not accessible to the public; however, the monument site is open daily and the Illinois Historic Preservation Agency honors the senator with special ceremonies to commemorate his birthday in April and his death in June. (Author's collection.)

SELF-GUIDED TOUR. Visitors to the Stephen A. Douglas monument, located at 636 East Thirty-fifth Street in Chicago's Bronzeville neighborhood, learn about the life of the senator through signs and photographs at the site. (Author's collection.)

Lack of funds caused construction to lag until an 1877 appropriation by the Illinois legislature revived the project. The column was raised in 1878 and topped by Volk's nine-foot statue of Douglas. Finishing touches came in 1881. Today, the senator's body rests in the sarcophagus of Vermont marble inscribed with his last words, "Tell my children to obey the laws and uphold the Constitution."

Laying the Douglas tomb cornerstone, September 6, ca. 1866.

BIBLIOGRAPHY

Andreas A. T. *History of Chicago from the Earliest Period to the Present Time*. Chicago: self-published, 1884.

Bernstein, Arnie. *The Hoofs and Guns of the Storm: Chicago's Civil War Connections*. Chicago: Lake Claremont Press, 2003.

Conneely, John. *The Family of Ellen Scully McLennan*. Chicago: self-published, 2001.

Cook, Frederick Francis. *Bygone Days in Chicago*. Chicago: A. C. McClurg and Company, 1910.

Greeley, Andrew M. *Irish Lace: A Nuala Anne McGrail Novel*. New York: Forge, 1996.

Levy, George. *To Die in Chicago, Confederate Prisoners at Camp Douglas 1862–1865*. Gretna, LA: Pelican Publishing Company, 1999.

McIlvaine, Mabel. *Reminiscences of Chicago During the Civil War*. New York: The Citadel Press, 1967.

INDEX

ACROSS AMERICA, PEOPLE ARE DISCOVERING SOMETHING WONDERFUL. *THEIR HERITAGE.*

Arcadia Publishing is the leading local history publisher in the United States. With more than 3,000 titles in print and hundreds of new titles released every year, Arcadia has extensive specialized experience chronicling the history of communities and celebrating America's hidden stories, bringing to life the people, places, and events from the past. To discover the history of other communities across the nation, please visit:

www.arcadiapublishing.com

Customized search tools allow you to find regional history books about the town where you grew up, the cities where your friends and family live, the town where your parents met, or even that retirement spot you've been dreaming about.